D1250702

Xenia Field's
Book of Garden
Flowers

*Perennials, Annuals and Biennials
and other attractive garden flowers*

Xenia Field's
Book of Garden
Flowers

HAMLYN
LONDON · NEW YORK · SYDNEY · TORONTO

ACKNOWLEDGEMENTS

We would like to thank Miss Joan Dove for creating the flower arrangements reproduced on pages 24 and 48 and Mrs. Sheila Macqueen for her arrangement on page 80. We would also like to thank the following photographers for the use of their pictures, in colour and black and white: *Amateur Gardening*, R. J. Corbin, Ernest Crowson of J. E. Downward, *The Field*, Valerie Finnis, Iris Hardwick, Peter Hunt, A. J. Huxley, Elsa M. Megson, Sheila Orme, Robert Pearson, Harry Smith and W. J. Unwin Ltd.

Published by
THE HAMLYN PUBLISHING GROUP LIMITED
LONDON · NEW YORK · SYDNEY · TORONTO
Hamlyn House, Feltham, Middlesex, England
© Xenia Field 1971
ISBN 0 600 01723 0
Printed in Italy by Arnoldo Mondadori, Verona
Photoset in England by V. Siviter Smith & Co. Ltd, Birmingham

Contents

A large part of this book has to do with herbaceous perennials, plants which have so much to offer present-day gardeners. But readers will know how impossible it is for perennials to keep the scene continuously colourful throughout the summer, and for this reason I have called in the annuals (hardy and half-hardy) and the biennials to fill the inevitable dull periods that are bound to arise.

This taste of summer flowers will, I hope, enable the beginner to see the picture as a whole.

It will be noticed that I have given some plants more space than others. These are, in my experience, those plants my readers have found difficult to grow. I hope the fuller information given will check the unsatisfactory number of early demises.

It will also be noticed that I have described some plants which do not fall in any of the categories mentioned above. In modern gardening no one group of plants can be treated in isolation, and these plants are included because they are often grown in association with those which come under my collective title Garden Flowers.

XENIA FIELD

Part One

Perennials

Getting Down to Earth

*Border Plant Troubles
(including those of
Annuals and Biennials)*

A Diversity of Borders

Selected Perennials

A colourful planting with *Achillea millefolium* Fire
King in the foreground, backed by blue
Geranium pratense flore pleno, grey artemisia and red
Astilbe Fanal, yellow verbascum and scarlet Sweet William

Getting Down to Earth
The Soil

Perennials are worthy garden plants and while enjoying good fare are not unduly greedy. Whatever the soil – heavy clay, over-light sand, chalk or hungry, polluted town soil – it is for the gardener to get out of it the best he can.

Treatment will depend on the type of soil, how it has been cultivated and what plants have been grown in it previously. The aim is to convert the land into fertile loam, and to concentrate on improving the top twelve inches of the soil, for it is within this top spit – as gardeners call it – that most plants feed.

Clay, wet and stubborn in winter and brick-hard in summer, presents a problem and entails hard work. But once broken down clay soil provides an excellent growing medium, although apt to be cold. Sandy and light soils are pleasant to work but need constant feeding with organic matter, manure, compost and so on to provide plants with a suitable diet. Lime dressings may be necessary, and few soils are averse to a taste of lime occasionally.

Chalk and gravel soils must be well broken down and mixed with manure, compost and peat, care being taken not to bring the sub-soil to the top. Peat soils are rare and situated in bog or fen country. They require draining, and lime dressings may be necessary to correct excessive acidity.

Soil is often improverished by previous crops and requires manuring. The addition of humus-forming material such as leafmould, compost, peat, etc. is necessary, however generous the gardener may be with fertilisers. It not only feeds, it retains moisture at the plants' roots and is the best way of putting back into the soil what has been taken out of it.

Drainage

Soil can be too wet for plant life to flourish or even survive. It can often be improved by trenching and filling the bottom of the trench with clinkers, coarse rubble and porous refuse that will absorb and help to clear any excessive moisture.

Faulty drainage makes itself apparent by tell-tale pools of water remaining on the surface of the soil for weeks without dispersing, while sick-looking plants droop and die. If further proof of waterlogging is needed, a few holes some 2 ft. deep should be dug in different parts of the garden. If these remain half or more full of water for long periods after heavy rainfall, then some form of drainage system is needed.

Fortunately, the majority of soils drain naturally, but clay soils are apt to suffer from unsatisfactory drainage and wet, sandy soil, though less common, is particularly difficult to drain. If waterlogging is serious and persistent then a sump hole or some form of piping or suitable tile drains will have to be laid. The herring-bone system of drainage entailing the use of large-sized land pipes that need to be buried at a certain depth and slope ($1\frac{1}{2}$ ft.– 3 ft. depending on the depth to which the soil is cultivated and sloping between 1 ft. in 20–40 ft.) calls for professional supervision.

A waterlogged soil will defeat the best of gardeners and it is essential to ensure an efficient runaway before cultivation is begun.

Digging

There is a theory – or maybe it is wishful thinking – that digging can be replaced by mulching. Whatever the rights of the argument may be, few gardeners have the quantity of mulching material, vegetable or kitchen waste which their garden would need. So dig we must.

Plain surface digging entails taking out the top spit (the 12 in. that are the depth of the spade) turning it over and replacing it. Double digging is the ideal if the gardener has the time and heart to work the soil to the depth of two spades.

Two stages in double digging: forking over the bottom of the trench and turning top spit soil over onto forked soil to leave both layers in their same relative positions

Enthusiastic sweet-pea fans obediently 'true' trench, taking out three spits to satisfy their plants. Whatever the method, it is all important to replace each layer of soil in its rightful place, the top spit to the top, the second spit below it, returning the deep spit to its original place and level. Clay soil demands autumn digging and the surface should be left rough so that the wind, rain and frost can break down the clods.

Digging is hard work best done at a measured pace, and energy should not be wasted by lifting the full spade higher than necessary. Only when movement becomes regular and rhythmic does digging become a pleasure.

The Compost Heap

Year by year a heavy tonnage of potential compost material is wasted. Refuse from kitchen or garden, in layers of 3 in. sandwiched between ordinary soil, makes lovely garden compost in a matter of months with the aid of a compost activator. Proprietary accelerators can be used to hasten decay; or alternatively, the fertiliser sulphate of ammonia can be dusted on the heap alternatively with dressings of hydrated lime. Make these alternate layers at 6-to 9-in. intervals as the heap is built up.

There are a few rules that are best kept. The heap should be limited in size to 5 ft. long, 4 ft. wide and at most 4 ft. high. It should be built up in an orderly manner, sloping the top or covering it with polythene to avoid excessive moisture and leaching from rain. In about one month's time the sides of the heap should be turned to the middle, the material being trodden down from time to time and, if necessary, watered occasionally, the aim being to keep the compost moist but not soggy.

Tough wood prunings from fruit trees or shrubs, evergreen clippings, conifers or roses, couch grass, ground elder, dandelion, bindweed and other persistent weeds are not suitable for the compost heap. Cabbage stumps should be cut up and lawn mowings added only in moderate

quantities at any one time as they engender excessive heat. Nor should lawn mowings be used if the grass has recently been treated with selective weedkiller.

It is all important that the heap should be well aerated. All dead organic matter will rot in time, but it is vital that while decomposing the air and sun should be free to get at the material, otherwise it may well putrify and become useless. A few holes made with a pointed stick, pushed well into the heap after the composting material has reached a few feet in height, will ensure the required ventilation.

After some months the compost will be ready for use–a decayed black-brown mass, crumbly and wholesome, the pride and joy of the veteran gardener. Encouraged, he will, no doubt, start another heap.

Overleaf: Bold sweeps of colour, skilfully combined, are always an asset in the garden. Here, the blue *Salvia superba*, yellow *Senecio przewalskii*, mauve *Phlox maculata alpha* and airy pink Thalictrum Hewitt's Double mix harmoniously

Manures and Fertilisers

Organic Manures

Half-decomposed manure, known as humus, is a blessing to the soil whether light or heavy, and as it decomposes so it is absorbed by plant roots. Horse manure, when well rotted and almost odourless, should be dug into the top 12 in. of soil in the autumn. When horse manure is not available, hop manure is a helpful substitute.

Poultry manure is strong stuff that must be kept under cover for at least six months before use and then be mixed with half to a third of dry soil. Some growers mix it with 10 times its bulk of granulated or moss peat with excellent results and I have found it a magical diet for sweet peas.

Peat, although of low nutrient value, is irreplaceable in holding water and improving the texture of the soil and has become one of the most popular mulches. Gardeners on light soil will find seaweed useful. It can be dug in during the autumn but is more easily laid on the top of the soil as a spring dressing.

The Needs of a Plant

Nitrogen. Lack of nitrogen shows itself in poor growth and stunted plants with pale foliage. The nitrogenous fertiliser hoof and horn is easy and clean to handle and has the advantage of acting slowly if a coarser grade is applied.

Phosphorus. Plants require phosphate to encourage flowering and healthy growth. An application of phosphates will often bring a dull, stationary plant into flower. Superphosphate of lime is quick-acting when raked in among the permanent residents of the border, and has a miraculous effect upon annuals if used at 1–2 oz. to each sq. yd. Bonemeal, safe and slow-acting, is the veteran's standby and is beneficial to all crops. Basic slag, also slow acting, is to be preferred for acid soils as it reduces the degree of acidity.

Potash. This alkaline substance increases the resistance of plants to disease and improves their colour ·and general performance. Sulphate of potash is probably the best fertiliser the amateur gardener can use. Applied at the rate of 1 oz. to each sq. yd. in the spring, followed by further doses later in the season, it works wonders.

The Two Types of Fertiliser

Organic fertilisers, which are of animal or vegetable origin, improve the soil while feeding the plants. Inorganic fertilisers, of mineral or chemical origin, are of great value but do not rejuvenate the soil, with the result that at some period humus will be required. I do not advise the gardener to join in the Cold War between the natural and the chemical, but to use both types with discretion.

Chemical–or, as they are often called, artificial–fertilisers are easy to handle in their modern form, but the gardener must have a care when using them, for some are extremely powerful. Reputable products are meticulously balanced by the manufacturers and should be used strictly according to instructions. The common tendency is to be over-generous when it is wiser to give too little rather than too much.

The pernickety gardener collects a host of tins and bottles in his desire to give each of his plants personal attention. The small gardener will find that a bag of general or 'complete' fertiliser of any reputable make will satisfy the majority of his plants. Such a fertiliser contains the three principal plant foods mentioned, namely, nitrogen, phosphorus and potash. As always it is difficult to please everybody, people or plants.

Mulching

Mulching is a valuable operation and Nature's way of feeding trees and plants. The fallen carpet of leaves not only provides nourishment but conserves moisture. The best time to mulch is in the spring as the plants wake up and just before the sap begins to rise. It should be done when the soil is thoroughly wet after rain or has been well soaked with a hose. A mulch should be spread on top of the surface soil in a generous circle, but be kept away from the stems of the plants. Summer mulching is helpful in keeping down weeds and

saves the gardener the chore of hoeing and frequent watering in dry spells. It should, however, be remembered that although a mulch slows down the loss of moisture, it also prevents rain reaching the soil. Periodically, the mulch should be drawn back and the soil given a soaking if this is found necessary.

Farmyard manure and peat are ideal mulches, and hop manure, vegetable refuse and any rotting material can be used. Lawn mowings should not be put on more than an inch thick, otherwise there is danger of generating too much heat. If a selective weedkiller has been used on the lawn, mowings must be kept for at least six months before being used.

Where a mulch has been applied, worms co-operate in the task of soil improvement, tugging the mulch down into the earth.

Planting

The majority of herbaceous plants are best planted in the autumn if the soil is light, and in the spring if it is heavy and the drainage poor. Spring planting is also advisable in town gardens if the atmosphere is impure. No effort should be spared in getting the soil in good condition before planting, so that the plant has a fair start and can be allowed to stay put for three or four years without disturbance.

Perennials should be planted in groups and it will be found easier to place an odd number effectively, three, five and seven or more plants, than an even number. Single specimens get lost in a large border and only the exotic yucca is capable of holding its own. More space should be allowed between the groups than between individual plants. When it comes to spacing it is important to know the habit of the plant, but as a rough guide I would suggest keeping small plants 7–8 in. and medium plants 15 in. apart, allowing 2 ft. between the tall subjects. The aim should be to hide the soil while avoiding over-crowding.

Plants should be carefully examined before planting, damaged roots being cut back with a sharp knife and any broken growths trimmed now rather than later. If the roots or root balls are desert-dry a soak in a pail of water before planting is helpful. A plant in a very dry state will find it difficult to absorb soil moisture.

The plants should be given holes deep and wide enough to allow their roots to be comfortably spread out without persuasion or 'cockling'. The position that will show the plant off to the best advantage has to be found; then, while the plant is held in one hand, soil can be trickled and finally drawn in with the other and firmly pressed down by hand or foot. It is vital to bring the roots into contact with the soil; air-pockets are a menace and responsible for many demises.

The size of the plant will determine whether a spade or trowel is best used for the operation. After planting, gardener and plants will appreciate a generous drink.

Propagation

Division

The easiest way to increase perennials is by division. The majority of them grow fast, adding to the clump from the centre outwards. The clump should be lifted in autumn or spring (in autumn in light soil, in spring in heavy). This splitting up is best done by driving two garden forks into the clump back to back, and pulling and teasing it first into two parts and then into smaller divisions. If this cannot be done with the hands then a knife can be used.

The young, lively growth that is wanted will be found round the outside of the clump and this should be replanted, the woody crown that is old and tired being discarded. When replanting, dig in well-rotted manure or peat and apply a dressing of bonemeal at about 4 oz. to each sq. yd.

On occasion in the spring it is possible to pull away a young shoot from the outside of a plant such as the delphinium with, it is hoped, a small root attached. The youngster can then be planted independently.

Softwood Cuttings

Many perennials, among them campanulas, lavatera, helianthemums and scabiosas, can be increased by softwood cuttings in spring and early summer. These cuttings, about 3 in. long, are best taken from low down on the plant. They should then be trimmed cleanly just below a node or joint with a sharp knife and the lower leaves removed.

Some gardeners root their cuttings in pure sand or vermiculite, repotting them into a suitable compost as soon as roots have formed, whereas others prefer to use a rooting mixture of one part medium loam, two parts peat and three parts sharp sand (all parts by bulk). The cuttings can either be inserted in pots or boxes placed in a propagating frame where a suitably moist, close atmosphere can be maintained, or be inserted directly into compost in a frame.

Cuttings are particularly vulnerable to loss of moisture until they have formed roots and shading should be given against direct sunshine. Spraying overhead with tepid water at intervals is necessary to keep the cuttings turgid.

Once rooted, they should be potted and placed in lighter, airier conditions to harden off gradually ready for planting in the border or nursery plot later on.

Root Cuttings

Some perennials with fleshy roots, such as the Oriental Poppies or verbascums, can be propagated by root cuttings taken in autumn or spring. Portions of root with an eye or slight swelling can be cut into pieces 1–3 in. long and planted vertically in a seed box using a sandy loam compost. These should be covered with an inch of compost, be given the protection of a frame, and watered only lightly until they begin to show some signs of life.

Layering Carnations and Pinks

Strong-jointed shoots of carnations and pinks that have not flowered can be layered from July to August by making a slanting cut half-way

Top: Stachys macrantha, a fine ground-cover plant, and other perennials
Bottom: The distinctive *Echinops ritro*, or Globe Thistle

through the stem with a sharp knife on the underside of the shoot just below a joint. The cut part of the stem must now be pressed down into a raised mound of sandy compost so that it is in close contact with the soil. The layer should then be pinned firmly in place with a hairpin and left to form roots. It should be ready for severing from the parent plant after six to seven weeks. The soil should be kept slightly moist throughout this period.

Seed

Numerous herbaceous plants, including, for example, the pyrethrum and aquilegia, can be raised from seed. They should be grown in the autumn or spring in open, sunny situations. A plant of this type may take three years to reach its zenith.

A 'rogue' seedling, one which is untrue to name, is the exception in a packet of seeds from a reputable nurseryman, but it should be understood that it is only species and certain varieties which will come true from home-saved seeds. Although there are many seed strains which breed practically true, to obtain an exact replica of a hybrid it is necessary to increase the plant vegetatively, such as by cuttings, division or layering.

Seed sowing is dealt with fully in the section on annuals (see p. 95).

Maintenance

Dead-heading

Plant life is highly concerned with regeneration. The short-lived annual is particularly anxious to reproduce itself and loses no opportunity of doing so. Flowering at the earliest moment, a seed pod is formed in double-quick time and once it swells the parent plant loses its youth and vigour and puts all its strength into reproduction. Flower will replace flower in the plant's endeavour to win the day. The gardener must indeed be watchful and pick off every faded flower—a task known as 'dead-heading'—if he is to keep his plants in

Top left: *Achillea filipendulina* Coronation Gold
Bottom left: *Convallaria majalis,*
the Lily-of-the-Valley

Top right: The statuesque Sea Holly,
Eryngium oliverianum
Bottom right: The April-flowering
Doronicum plantagineum excelsum

21

bloom until the frosts arrive. A single spent head is a victory for the plant.

Weeds

If the gardener can deal with the fibrous-rooted weeds by hoeing before they flower he will save himself much labour later on. Tap-rooted kinds, among them the dandelion, couch grass and ground elder, defeat the hoe and are best poisoned by 'painting' a weed-killing chemical on the leaves, or removed by hand weeding. Unfortunately, even if buried at great depth they manage to survive. Thistles are prickly horrors that can be forked out; bindweed is best dealt with by dangling the top growth in a jam-jar of a chemical such as 2,4,5-T with 2,4-D; oxalis is a modern menace against which we have not, as yet, an effective control.

Garden weedkillers, becoming more efficient every year, are a great help. Paraquat acts on the foliage and stems of the plants with which it comes in contact but becomes inactive on touching the soil and can be safely used among plants in beds and borders, provided these are not touched by the chemical. Annual broad-leaved weeds are killed by this chemical and also the top growth of perennial weeds and grasses. Simazine, an effective control for many germinating weeds, remains active in the soil for months on end but does not spread laterally; it is an excellent weed-killer for paths and drives. Our old friend sodium chlorate remains the best total weedkiller we have, provided the soil can be left vacant for at least six months after its use. It should be used strictly in accordance with the manufacturer's directions and, like all garden chemicals, be kept locked away from children.

Staking

The gardener is often told to stake with discretion; this is much easier said than done. The Floppy plant that, in old English, is in need of 'some supportance' should be staked while still small, to spare it from damage, from storm and from rain. Wind is apt to rock the tall and newly planted

and if staking is left until later in the season, the supports are more difficult to camouflage.

Pea-sticks provide useful support and are easily hidden, but plants with heavier stems, such as delphiniums, will need individual stakes that attract less attention if painted green.

Watering

There is one golden rule when watering; be generous and make it a good soak. Dribs and drabs merely bring thirsty roots to the surface without satisfying them, and do more harm than good. The newly planted will benefit from a good watering in, and in the case of more delicate plants a mulch of peat after this watering may be a life-saver.

Autumn Renovation

When autumn comes, the border should be tidied up. There are trespassers and smotherers that must be restrained, cut back and kept in place. The soil can be lightly forked over, care being taken not to injure surface roots.

Dead foliage may be cut to the ground in warm southern gardens, but in cold gardens it is safer to trim only lightly, leaving the die-back to act as a protection against wind and frost.

The Three-year Cycle

Every three or four years the herbaceous border needs a thorough overhaul in spring or autumn, but there are certain plants such as the lilies, peonies and *Alstroemeria* Ligtu Hybrids that abhor disturbance and must be left in peace and given a feed *in situ*.

The majority of clumps will require splitting up (see p. 18 for details of division) and this is an opportunity to treat the lime-lovers to a taste of hydrated lime. The more tender plants also need a light covering of well-weathered ashes in autumn, before the severe weather arrives. Autumn-planted perennials may be 'lifted' by severe frost and it is wise to watch for this through the winter and make them firm again before growth starts in the spring.

Border Plant Troubles

Some Pests

Perennials, biennials and annuals are all attacked by pests and diseases from time to time, but on the whole rather less than many other plants. The weak, sickly, starved and emaciated plants are particularly vulnerable and invite the enemy. If the gardener is meticulous in burning discoloured and unhealthy leaves and rotting debris, and maintains a high standard of hygiene in the border, he will reduce the incidence of both pests and diseases.

Ants

These small insects damage the roots of young plants by underground tunnelling and nest making. They are often lured into the border in their search for honeydew excreted by the aphids. Nests can be destroyed by pouring boiling water over them, by dusting the nests with BHC or derris, or by applying Nippon which, when carried back to the nest by the ants, acts as a mass destroyer.

Aphids

Greenfly is the most universal of all garden pests, and some plants, among them the nasturtium, are menaced by blackfly. They are readily controlled by malathion, but the novice must be reminded that this spray is harmful both to bees and fish. Menazon, derris (very poisonous to fish but harmless to humans and animals) and pyrethrum (non-poisonous to humans and warm-blooded animals) will also combat this pest.

Birds

Crocus and polyanthus and, more recently, wisteria, are attacked by birds and there is no complete protection against their onslaught. A spray with Morkit–a bird repellent chemical–is helpful, but unfortunately a heavy shower will wash the solution away making a second treatment necessary. The unsatisfactory alternatives, black cotton and twig wigwams or barricades, are time consuming to erect and detract from the glamour of the flowers they defend, while birds chirp fearlessly at flapping scarers and ugly bits of glitter and soon become indifferent to them.

Caterpillars

The larvae of butterflies and moths may be sprayed or dusted with derris and any survivor dealt with by finger and thumb.

Cats

The cat is a squatter; it sits, sleeps and suns itself while flattening out its favourite plant and few subjects survive this treatment. It would appear the cat has no liking for the strong smell of ammonia, and it might well pay the gardener to sprinkle the cat's haunt with this liquid just before siesta time. A sniff of ammonia plus a bedding of prickly thistle or holly leaves has induced many a puss to desert its seat.

Cuckoo Spit

This is the larvae–yellow or green in colour–of the froghopper and not a serious pest. It can be quickly cleared by first removing the spittle with water and afterwards spraying with derris.

Dogs

There are various proprietary dog repellents available that vary in their effectiveness in keeping dogs at bay, including a specially treated cord.

Earwigs

These pests are specially damaging to the dahlia. Earwigs eat at night and can be trapped in upturned pots filled with hay, placed on canes above the plant, and shaken out over a bucket of

Collerette dahlias arranged with sedum,
eryngium, astrantia and variegated holly by Joan Dove

water in the morning. Earwigs and woodlice can also be controlled by applications of BHC.

Eelworms

These small creatures are not visible to the naked eye and it is almost impossible to eradicate them. All affected plants must be burnt and the gardener should avoid replanting the species on the same ground for at least three years. Phlox, chrysanthemums, primulas and campanulas are plants which are particularly vulnerable to damage by these pests.

Slugs

There are a number of metaldehyde and bran products available in different forms which are capable of attracting and poisoning this beastly pest. A dressing of sharp cinders makes progress uncomfortable for slugs.

Some Diseases

Black Spot on Roses

Maneb controls both black spot on roses and rust and many rosarians prefer this product to captan (I mention this here because roses are often nowadays grown in association with perennial and other border plants).

Chlorosis

This is a physiological ailment resulting in the yellowing of foliage due to a deficiency of chlorophyll. A generous feed of organic manure will usually put the matter right, particularly if a shortage of iron is suspected.

Damping off

Seedlings under glass are vulnerable to stem rot at the point where the seedlings meet the soil. A box of seedlings may succumb to damping off within a few hours due to wet soil, soggy conditions, lack of ventilation or drought. If John Innes Seed Compost or sterilised soil is used for seed sowing the risk of disease is minimised. Some gardeners treat the soil with Cheshunt

Compound as a safeguard, both before sowing and at pricking out time.

I am often asked to describe the term 'buoyant atmosphere', so often advised by experts in relation to the greenhouse. Roughly speaking, it is a pleasant and comfortable atmosphere that the gardener would himself appreciate – fresh rather than stuffy, with plenty of ventilation but no draughts.

Mildew

The leaves of mildew-affected plants become twisted and covered with a powdery white coating that attacks soft growth in the autumn, often as a result of rapid and excessive changes in temperature. The affected parts of the leaves gradually turn from white to brown as the disease progresses. Mildew is capable of overwintering in the soil and is a killer if allowed to go unchecked.

Roses and Michaelmas daisies suffer badly from this sickness, but a dusting or spray with some form of sulphur, or a spray with Karathane (dinocap) immediately the attack is spotted and repeated at ten-day or fortnightly intervals, should keep the disease at bay.

Virus Diseases

Dahlias, petunias, zinnias, nasturtiums and many other border plants suffer from a virus that travels in the 'bloodstream' (sap) of the plants, often causing widespread destruction and resulting in strange distortions or markings. Many of the 'wilt' conditions are due to the presence of virus, for which there is no known cure. All plants suffering severely from the disease are best burnt and a constant watch kept for aphids that so often act as virus 'carriers'.

A Warning

Care should be taken when using insecticides and fungicides not to overdose the plants. In my experience this is a common fault. Even more important, keep all insecticides and fungicides locked away, especially if there are children in the family.

A Diversity of Borders

Borders can be of any length, broad or narrow, straight or winding. I advise the beginner against the very narrow border of less than 6 ft. in width which has a thin and skimpy look, and does not allow the plants sufficient room or the gardener sufficient scope. If the border faces south then almost anything will grow, but for north-facing borders a more careful selection is required.

The True Herbaceous Border

Such borders were for many years almost sacred institutions kept strictly to herbaceous plants, the hardy perennials. (True herbaceous plants have a life-span of over two years, die down to the ground in late autumn and throw up fresh growth each spring.) Often extensive and very beautiful, this sort of planting demanded more attention and money than has been generally available for many years. The regimented border so carefully planted according to height, each clump and stem meticulously in its allotted place, has been largely replaced (although superb examples can still be seen in some public gardens and in some private gardens opened to the public) by the mixed and labour-saving border.

The Mixed Border

With the arrival of the mixed border the gardener was liberated. He was allowed to introduce the gaiety of spring bulbs, the daffodils, tulips and scillas; the brilliance of the annuals; the telling shapes and textures of shrubs, the dark green Irish Yew *(Taxus baccata fastigiata),* the glaucous silver pyramids of the juniper and the fascinating, spiky yucca. Monotony was defeated and there was now the grace and scent of roses to provide an additional attraction. Gradation of height was no longer of account. A hollyhock might find itself in the front line and giants and creepers march together. The flowering season was as a result happily prolonged, the gardener might please himself and the sky was the limit.

The Double-sided Border

This border is dominated by a bold centrepiece. As in the case of the mixed border the surrounding plants need not be strictly herbaceous. If the border is comparatively small then heights should be restricted and very tall hollyhocks and six-footers would be out of balance and place.

A keen plantsman, anxious for the welfare of his plants, will show a preference for the double-sided border or open site, free from a background of overhanging trees or hedges and the hungry roots of large chestnuts, yew or privet. He shuns the desert-dry conditions of the old, pink brick wall, preferring the open site provided it is not too windswept.

The One-sided Border

This planting may have a shrubbery, hedge, fence or wall in the background, a telling backcloth, that will show off the border flowers. A gardener should be ready to put up with a few leaching roots and loss of moisture and richness from the soil in return for a fine old yew hedge as a background. After all, aggressive roots can be cut back every few years and an extra dollop of manure dug into the soil.

A tall wall or a thick evergreen hedge can be detrimental to the plants and they can be seen leaning away in resentment from the overpowering shade. But some will benefit by the protection against unfriendly weather and will flower earlier as a result.

Again, the width of the border is important. The more dominant the backcloth the wider the border should be, and some very tall plants will be wanted. Massive drifts of delphiniums, verbascums and kniphofias are always very effective in the rear.

A slab-paved path, of at least 2 ft. in width, between the shrubbery or hedge is a 'must', providing air and light for the plants and access and elbow-room for the working gardener. In

Top: A well-groomed hedge makes a telling backcloth for border flowers
Bottom: Mixed borders in which different categories of plants are grown together, as shown here, are very much a part of the modern garden

late June, if a dull period occurs, there should be no scruple in filling up the gaps with bulbs and annuals, or even a shrub or two, where they are called for.

The Mini-border

The mini or midget border has become fashionable largely due to the enthusiasm of Mr. Alan Bloom of Bressingham Gardens, Diss, Norfolk. It is suitable for the small or windswept garden and the gardener who has little time for staking.

Achillea Moonshine, *Anaphalis triplinervis, Campanula* Purple Pixie, *Dianthus* Isolde, *Geum borisii, Potentilla* Gibson's Scarlet and *Sedum spectabile* Autumn Joy, are a few from a host of possibles for use in such a garden feature.

The Special or Hobby-plant Border

Rose borders there are in plenty; in America I saw two memorable iris borders and a superb lily border. The tall bearded iris and the peony both make excellent collector's plants.

By introducing a number of different varieties of the chosen genus, the flowering season can be prolonged, but the specialist has to be prepared to face long uneventful off-seasons. The most lovely one-plant border I have come across is the fairy-like aquilegia border at the National Trust garden at Polesden Lacey, Dorking, Surrey.

Effective borders can be confined to two favourite flowers. I can recommend a tall, white iris border with a backing of apricot lupins. On occasion I have found a fern border cool and restful in the heat of the day, coming after a surfeit of dazzling bedders and annuals.

The Single-colour Border

The white border led the way, then came the blue border, followed by the pink and yellow borders; and the dazzling red border, which was the last to be introduced. A red and orange planting which I saw in Scotland, not far from Montrose, was rich and garish and remains vivid in my mind. It is said that flowers cannot clash, but I have

Top: The handsome, variegated-leaved *Hosta undulata* plays an important role both in the foliage border and the front of a shrubbery
Bottom: Plants which flower in autumn are especially desirable, including rose-salmon *Sedum* Autumn Joy shown here

caught the vermilion hybrid tea rose Super Star violently disagreeing with an orange alstroemeria.

It is well worth remembering that famous gardener Gertrude Jekyll's tip that strong warm colours need the foil of gradually intermingling shades, and that the cool colours and pure blue especially demand a contrast.

The Foliage Border

A planting of over 30 different varieties of hostas shown by The Royal Horticultural Society at a recent Chelsea Flower Show illustrated how effective a foliage border can be. Variegated plants always hold my attention, but enthusiastic collectors will find many grey, silver or glaucous-leaved plants that certainly deserve a place in such a border.

Hostas, with their strong leaves of grand architectural quality and interesting flowers, look extremely well planted in front of the beautiful *Acanthus mollis* and some of the euphorbias or spurges would not be out of place in this setting, especially if there is rough ground to cover. *Euphorbia marginata,* an annual, with green and silver striped leaves and white bracts, will seed itself generously if happy with you, and *Thymus* Gold Queen or Silver Queen will fill a corner.

The Seasonal Border

Gardeners who are away from home in August, through the winter months or at any particular time of the year will plant accordingly. June, July and August are the 'glut' months for perennial plants.

The autumn border is more free flowering than the spring border, but there are more shrubs early in the year to keep the overall picture colourful than in the autumn, for not many shrubs flower after July.

The Flower Arranger's Border

Few gardeners willingly agree to their flowers being cut for house decoration. A special garden

Top: Primula denticulata, the Drumstick Primula, a reliable and gallant little plant that heralds the arrival of spring
Bottom: A splendid ground-cover plant, *Alchemilla mollis*, Lady's Mantle, beloved by the flower arranger

for the flower arranger, where he or she may use the knife fancy free, and grow not only the beautiful but the comic, odd and peculiar, will give pleasure and may avoid argument.

The Alpine and Rock Plant Border

Creeping ground huggers and plants that carpet the soil are quite happy without rocks to climb. All these plants need is a good soil and a cool root run. Aubrietas, campanulas, dianthus, heucheras, saxifrages and stonecrops (sedums) are reliable stand-bys. The alpine meadow, lawn or border – if possible a trifle sloped – is delightful.

The Scented Border

The aroma of sweet-scented flowers for some is nostalgic. Many have a special attraction for the gardener, others are magnetic to the bee.

Cheiranthus, dianthus, monardas, peonies and verbenas have a strong fragrance but it is the phloxes above all other perennials that fill the air with scent.

The Shady Border

The majority of plants demand light all day if they are to flower. But there are some like the hellebores, doronicum, dicentra, lily-of-the-valley, foxgloves, Solomon's seal, Japanese anemones and the primula family that are happy in semi-shade and shade.

The sunless border has no need to be flowerless and dreary if the nurseryman's list for the shady garden is consulted.

The Ground-cover Border

The gardener without time and only a small budget should turn to the ground-cover border. *Bergenia cordifolia,* the useful Elephant's Ears; *Campanula poscharskyana,* with bright green foliage and profuse light blue flowers in summer and early autumn; *Tiarella cordifolia,* the Foam Flower, with fluffy cream-white flowers; *Alchemilla mollis* or Lady's Mantle, with sulphur-green flowers, and others on the ground-cover list will give a wonderful return for little trouble.

29

Selected Perennials

Acanthus (Bear's Breeches). This handsome plant was much admired by the Greeks and Romans and was their inspiration in decorating the Corinthian pillars. The tubular flowers are a dull pink or white suffused rose and are borne on stiff spikes in late summer. The leaves are large and thistle-like.

This classical plant likes a well-drained deep loam and flowers freely in a sunny position. Newly planted specimens should be given protection until established. It is a good town plant and I have seen it particularly well planted down the centre of a long narrow bed in a garden in a Kensington square in association with *Hosta undulata*—a delightful plantain lily with bright green leaves—and blocks of Cambridge Blue lobelias.

Acanthus mollis is the most commonly grown species. But the white *A. m. latifolius* and purplish *A. spinosus* with grey foliage have the same classical charm.

Propagation of these plants is by seed or division in spring.

Achillea (Milfoil, Yarrow). A fine group of flat-headed, yellow, tansy flowers held on stiff silvery stems that have a great attraction for the butterfly; the plant's only requirements are good soil and plenty of sunshine. It is a long time since Achilles discovered the medicinal properties of the achillea, which possesses over a hundred species and a number of striking hybrids, from the 6-in. rock plant *A. clavennae,* with silvery foliage and white flowers (which appear in May and June), to varieties of the *A. filipendulina* that grow to over 4 ft. Gold Plate and Coronation Gold bear impressive golden platters some 7 in. across in July and August. Gathered just before their zenith and hung upside down in an airy place, the dried heads will last the winter through in flower arrangements.

Achillea millefolium is the wild Yarrow and the red Fire King, 2 ft., and Cerise Queen, 3 ft., are the best garden forms. These flower in July and August.

Of the flat-headed achilleas I like the quieter pale lemon-yellow *A. taygetea*, 2 ft., and the silvery-foliaged Moonshine, both of which are easy, long-lasting plants suitable for a sunny mini-border and flowering from June to September.

Achillea ptarmica, 2 ft., the Sneezewort, with white button flowers that come in clusters, is an accommodating plant but a potential trespasser that must be kept in place. The Pearl is a useful cutting variety, flowering from June to August.

Achilleas are readily increased by division in spring or autumn but the gardener must have a care and grow the superior varieties only. Cuttings can also be taken in early summer.

African Lily see Agapanthus.

Agapanthus (African Lily). These grand plants from South Africa are, in the same way as the camellias, sturdier than the Victorians suspected. During the last century they spent most of their time in the conservatory, but we have learned since that on a well-drained soil they can survive 30 degrees of frost, and in the south and mild areas may be considered hardy. Nevertheless, a light dressing of bracken or straw in severe weather will not come amiss.

The circular heads of bloom on strong stems are of varying blues or white, and the leaves strong and strap-like. Any reasonably good, well-drained soil and a sheltered position is suitable, and spring planting normally advised.

Agapanthus africanus (also known as *A. umbellatus mooreanus*) is deep blue with a full umbel of flowers in summer, 20 in., while *A. campanulatus* is slightly shorter and of a powdery sky blue colour, flowering freely during July and August. *A. orientalis* (syn. *A. umbellatus*) bears umbels of deep blue flowers on 3-ft. stems in late summer and autumn; there are various forms available including a white-flowered, a double-flowered and a variegated variety.

The Headbourne Hybrids are newcomers that have been evolved from the Hon. Lewis Palmer's collection made in the higher regions of South Africa. They have proved far more hardy than any we have known previously, and came through the severe winters of 1961 and 1962 in many parts of the country without protection. It can be fairly said that these hybrids are hardy grown in well-drained soil in the South of England. They are to be had in varying shades of blue and flower in July and August.

The agapanthus is one of the most satisfactory tub plants we possess.

Propagation is easy, the plants being divided in March. Also by seed, but plants so raised are slow to flower.

Ajuga (Bugle). This dwarf plant, with spikes of mostly blue flowers in summer, has come into fashion as a ground-cover plant. It is an easily grown, undemanding subject.

Ajuga pyramidalis is one of the most attractive species with gentian-blue flowers, but it is *A. reptans variegata* that is in the limelight as a ground-cover plant. The green leaves are edged and bespattered with creamy yellow and the plant travels fast by means of throwing out a series of runners. *A. r. atropurpurea*, with purple-bronze foliage, makes a luxurious carpet for orange lilies.

The humble little bugle of the field has now been promoted to the garden. All those referred to are about 6 in. in height.

Propagation is simple, by division in spring or autumn, or by seed sown in spring.

Alchemilla (Lady's Mantle). This is an unassuming little plant, loved and publicised by the late Constance Spry, the distinguished flower arranger. It is still to be found growing wild in the North of England and in Scotland. The small, greenish-straw-coloured flowers are individually unimportant, but when massed together in loose sprays are delightfully decorative. Easy to please, this plant requires a well-drained but moist soil.

Alchemilla mollis, 18 in., displays masses of tiny green-sulphur flowers in loose sprays in summer, and is beloved of the flower arranger; the kidney-shaped leaves are hairy and borne on long stalks.

This plant is increased by division in spring or seed sown outdoors in spring.

Allium. There are 280 known species of garlic, these including our culinary onion. The ornamental species have small flowers massed together in globular heads solid or tasselled, and come in a wide range of colours—sky blue, purple, lilac and rose-pink. A sunny position and a well-drained ordinary soil are their only demands. They should be planted from October to November covering the bulbs with soil to a depth of twice their diameter.

Allium sphaerocephalum, 1–2 ft., with a deep purple dense head is a useful addition to the July–August border, with *A. albopilosum*, 1 ft., a native of Turkestan with a mop-head of small lilac stars making a charming mauve-green cobweb, is excellent for cutting.

Propagation is by the offsets which the plants produce freely, in autumn or spring. Also by bulbils and seeds sown in March.

Alstroemeria (Peruvian Lily, that comes from Chile!). *Alstroemeria aurantiaca*, with orange trumpet flowers and leafy stems, is slow to settle down but once established is quite difficult to eradicate. I admire the way it survives in old and neglected herbaceous borders, refusing to be starved out.

The improved forms, Dover Orange and Moerheim Orange, both 3 ft., are fine plants, and make a splendid feature in the July border. The gardener will have to be a little careful in choosing associates for the orange Peruvian Lily for it is an awkward mixer. It is, as a rule, happiest with white or blue flowers as neighbours.

When, 25 years or more ago, the beautiful 3–4 ft. pink, coral and flame to orange Ligtu Hybrids made their appearance, they were an immediate hit. They are lovely things, also flowering in June and July, but unfortunately the majority of gardeners have found them difficult to establish. The easiest way would seem to be to grow them from seed in large pans, either in the spring or soon after the seed has been harvested, sowing as thinly as possible so that the seedlings

Below: *Alstroemeria* Ligtu Hybrids, beautiful but often a little difficult to establish. This plant demands a rich, well-drained soil and a warm position

can be left undisturbed for the first year. Some gardeners prefer to sow the seeds in small peat pots, one to each pot, and later planting out the seedlings in their pots in the border. Pot plants are preferable when buying as they can be planted out with less root disturbance.

The Ligtu Hybrids require a rich, well-drained soil and a warm position. They must be given a light covering of straw to protect them in the winter, at least for the first year or two when they are particularly vulnerable. Even when established, in cold parts of the country their young shoots should be given light straw or twiggy protection when they come through the soil.

These beautiful hybrids are worth the attention they demand when newly planted and in youth.

Propagation is by seed, as already explained, or by division in March or September–October.

Alum-root, see Heuchera

Alyssum (Madwort, Gold Dust). *Alyssum saxatile,* a showy yellow or golden plant with silvery foliage, is a woody and persistent rock plant, too

often seen in the company of the mauve aubrieta and white rock cress (arabis). It is a sturdy perennial for the front of the border, giving an early spring show when there are few flowers about. Ordinary good soil and an open position and firm pruning are the only requirements of this easygoing plant.

Alyssum saxatile flore pleno is a sturdy, double-flowered, gold, long-lasting plant of 6–9 in. Among the less brash and, to my mind, more pleasing, are the primrose-yellow Silver Queen and the buff Dudley Neville. These flower during May and June. *A. spinosum roseum* is a modest plant seen less often, that makes dense grey bushes smothered with pink flowers from June to August. This plant is now listed in some catalogues as *Ptilotrichum spinosum roseum*.

Propagation is by seed sown either in frames in March or the open garden in April, or by half-ripe cuttings, preferably rooted in a frame during early summer.

Anaphalis (Pearl Everlasting). This is a grey-

Bottom left: The friend of countless gardeners: *Alyssum saxatile*, which is valuable for its early-spring display
Bottom right: The grey-foliaged, white-flowered Pearl Everlasting, *Anaphalis nubigena*

foliaged plant with grouped heads of white, rounded or starry flowers that can be bunched and dried as everlasting flowers. It is an easy-going plant with a dislike for drought, but good drainage is necessary.

Anaphalis nubigena, 8 in., with bright foliage, and *A. triplinervis*, 15 in., that has attractive white woolly leaves are useful for autumn arrangements. *A. yedoensis*, 2 ft., with erect silvery growth and tidy, semi-everlasting flowers, has a place in the white border.

Propagation is by seed sown in a cold frame in spring. Also by division in spring or autumn.

Anchusa (Bugloss). This showy, blue-flowering perennial in shades of light to deep blue, with coarse foliage and grey stems is a joy in early summer. Anchusas enjoy ordinary well-drained soil and a sunny border and should be given plenty of elbow room. They may be planted from October to March. It is worth remembering, too, that they are over-generous flowerers and, unless controlled, may well flower to death.

Anchusa caespitosa, a bright gentian-blue species, 12–15 in., is most desirable and flowers from May to July, but is not, unfortunately, very long lived. A better proposition perhaps for most gardens are the varieties of *A. azurea* such as the deep blue Dropmore, the bright blue Morning Glory, pale blue Opal, mid-blue Pride of Dover, Royal Blue, and gentian-blue Loddon Royalist, a variety that manages without staking. These are all first rate, ranging from 3–6 ft. and flowering from late May to July or August.

I am particularly fond of associating the paler of the anchusas with the pale pink *Pyrethrum* May Queen.

Propagation is by seed sown in a frame in March or in the open ground in May. Anchusas can also be increased by division of the roots in March, or by root cuttings inserted in sandy soil in winter. Propagation is something of a challenge. Root cuttings would seem to be more in the hands of the gods than the gardener, and the progeny of seeds are more likely to be variable than true.

But young plants are essential, being more virile than the old.

Anemone (Windflower). The well-known Japanese anemone, *Anemone japonica* (or *A. hupehensis*), is the important late-summer to autumn-flowering member of this group. The flowers are saucer shaped and carried high above the vine-like foliage. There are white, rose, mauve, suffused wine-red and purple varieties, a number of them being semi-double, borne on 2½-ft. stems. They are unfussy about soil and I have seen anemones nobly flowering from August to October in a sunless, dank town garden. Anemones are best introduced to the garden in the spring, and are sensitive to disturbance.

Anemone lesseri is similar in flower formation to *A. japonica*, but it is a shorter species of 1 ft. which bears carmine flowers in May and June. There are other members of the family, such as *A. vitifolia,* 2 ft., with white flowers in July, that are valuable in the wild border, where they may be allowed to spread.

The amateur gardener, however, is mainly interested in the named varieties described in catalogues as Japanese anemones. These are splendid plants for autumn colour. For example, Bressingham Glow, 2 ft., a semi-double, rosy red, heads my list; Lady Gilmour, 2 ft., an almost double pink that hangs its head becomingly; and Louise Uhink, 3½ ft., is one of the finest whites. These three planted together make a delightful trio.

The anemones make ideal companions for the hardy fuchsias. I have only one complaint about them—they droop immediately when cut. Maybe if they were more difficult to grow they would be treated with more respect.

Propagation is by seed sown in sandy soil in a frame in spring, by division after flowering or by root cuttings in autumn or spring.

Anthemis (Chamomile, Golden Marguerite). The anthemis is a plant known for its medicinal properties. There are some fine perennials among the members of this daisy-like family, both single and double, in white and different shades of yellow. The foliage is elegant and scented.

Willing to grow in an ordinary well-drained soil, this sun lover blooms right through the summer. It must be cut down after flowering so that it may make new growth for cuttings before severe weather arrives.

The chamomile is well worth growing and the named varieties of *A. tinctoria* are excellent plants, and good for cutting. The golden-yellow Grallagh Gold, bright yellow Perry's Variety and the sulphur-yellow Wargrave Variety, all 2½ ft. and flowering from June to September, are my choice from a long list. Double varieties are on the way.

Perhaps I should put in a word for the yellow *A. rudolphiana*, 9–10 in., as dianthus lovers like to grow the silver, feathery foliage with their pinks.

Increase by division in March is to be preferred to raising plants from seed as the latter method usually produces a high proportion of 'rogues'; also by half-ripe cuttings rooted in summer in a cold frame.

Aquilegia (Columbine). Fairy-like, spurred flowers on slender stalks in blue and white, crimson and gold and many self colours, dancing in the breeze like ballerinas, are an entrancing picture from May to June. No wonder Durer never tired of drawing them. The spurs, one of the great attractions of these plants, vary in length and some measure more than the flower itself. This is a happy plant provided there are no excesses in the form of drought or waterlogging. It tolerates partial shade and lasts longer if protected from full sun.

There are a number of dwarfs and my pick of these are *A. alpina*, with Wedgwood-blue flowers on 1-ft. stems in May, that sows itself with abandon, and *A. glandulosa*, 9–12 in., with blue and white flowers in May and June. But it is the long-spurred hybrids offered by nurserymen, many the outcome of unknown crosses, that attract attention. Crimson Star and Blue King, both 1½ ft., are favourites, while the Dragonfly dwarfs and Mrs. Scott-Elliott's long-spurred hybrids have made a name for themselves. Even more impressive are the McKana Hybrids with large, very long-spurred flowers on 3-ft. stems.

The plants cross themselves and set seed freely but the chance crosses are likely to be inferior to their parents. Even carefully collected seed from a reputable source is apt to result in a high percentage of rogues.

Lastly, a sad truth, Columbines, or if you prefer it, Granny's Bonnet or Doves-round-a-Dish, are short-lived plants rarely surviving for four years, if as long.

Propagation is by seed sown in a frame in August or in a semi-shaded seed bed in May or June. Veteran plants may be divided in March or April but the gardener should have a care for the aquilegia has long tap-roots and resents disturbance. For this reason seedlings should be transferred to their flowering positions as soon as they can be comfortably handled.

Arabis (Rock Cress). Arabis is a white, grey-foliaged single or double rampant grower that needs a firm hand. However, it makes an effective display in spring and is undemanding, asking only for a sunny position and ordinary garden soil. The double form, *Arabis albida flore pleno,* is a doubtful stayer, frequently reverting to single flowers and maybe because of this shortcoming is becoming scarce. There are also pink (*A. a. rosa-bella)* and pleasant variegated (*A. a. variegata)* forms.

The single varieties are increased by cuttings in a shady border in summer, also by seed sown in cold frames in early spring and division when flowering has finished. Double varieties are increased by division and cuttings.

Armeria (Thrift, Sea Pink). The armerias have rounded heads of pink flowers and grassy foliage. Willing doers and happy seaside plants, they will grow in the poorest of sandy soils. *Armeria maritima* is a wild flower still to be seen on some parts of the coast. The pick of the family is the reddish-pink variety Vindictive which flowers from late May to July.

Armeria caespitosa with light pink flowers on 4-in. stems from April to June, and *A. plantaginea* Bee's Ruby, 2 ft., with bright ruby-red flowers deserve a place.

Propagation is by seed sown in sandy soil in spring or by division of roots in early autumn or spring.

Artemisia (Wormwood, Southernwood). The artemisia is a feathery, bushy, rather coarse grey-green foliaged plant, shrubby and aromatic, with unimportant flowers. Some artemisias like the sun more than others; all demand a well-drained soil. They have come to the fore with the advent of the silver foliage border and for this reason I give a fairly full list.

Artemisia abrotanum Lambrook Silver, 3 ft., is one of the most impressive of the family, with cascading silver leaves. The shrubby *A. arborescens,* a shimmering, silky, silver-foliaged subject for the back of the border is a splendid companion for delphiniums. It varies considerably in height to a maximum of 3½ ft. The lacy foliage of *A. nutans,* 3 ft., also shrubby, looks well grown cheek by jowl with Love-in-a-Mist. *A. ludoviciana,* 2–4 ft., a grey-white, willow-leaved plant with slender, erect stems, bears plumes of tiny off-white flowers which are of little consequence. Artemisias look particularly lovely growing among white or deep red roses.

Propagation is by division in the spring, except in the case of the shrubby subjects that can be increased by cuttings in sandy soil in a frame during early summer.

Aster (Michaelmas Daisy). The perennial asters or Michaelmas daisies are hardy, will grow in town or country, and are gay, prolific, easy to grow and cheap to buy. Year by year I beg gardeners to throw away their wishy-washy Michaelmas daisies and replace them with the splendid modern varieties. It is an uphill battle.

No flower can look more dejected than the pre-war, worn out, miserable mauve aster. Many gardens lose colour and interest once the roses and annuals have said goodbye. Now that the aster has snapped out of its drabness, it can join the dahlia in keeping the border lively.

This is a plant that will grow in almost any soil and situation but it deserves deeply dug soil to which well-rotted manure has been added.

Having invested in a few new varieties, the gardener will no doubt wish to grow the plant in the new manner. If fine spikes and sprays are wanted for exhibition the number of stems allowed to develop from a single rootstock must be strictly limited. The gardener need not be as strict as the showman, but I advise his contenting himself with three or four stems and keeping the clumps small.

When it comes to dividing the plants the strong outside growth will make a generous number of young plants and the tired centre can be discarded.

It is important to keep stock young and virile. Newly planted specimens should not be allowed to dry out before they have anchored themselves in the soil. Those who garden on sandy soil should plant firmly and be ready with the watering-can. Spring is the safest time for planting.

Alas, aster wilt is prevalent in some areas and the grower should watch for wilt symptoms—flagging from the base of the plants upwards and, in advanced stages, the formation of white fungus on the stem at soil level. All affected plants should be removed immediately and burnt.

The aster is extremely vulnerable to mildew and few varieties are immune. Affected plants are best treated with green sulphur dust. The gardener who dusts as a preventive measure from mid-summer onwards scores over those who wait until the trouble has become widespread. Aphids can be a menace; they are difficult to spot for they feed inside the tightly rolled leaves which surround the tips of the new growth.

Well over a hundred asters are listed in specialist herbaceous plant catalogues and I have had difficulty in confining myself to a list of reasonable length.

Aster amellus: the varieties belonging to this species have large flowers with prominent gold centres, and bloom from August to October. The colours include pink, lavender, violet, purple, and various shades of blue. The foliage is slightly grey. These plants grow on a woody rootstock and are stalwarts, staking as a rule being unnecessary. The

Top left: Bergenia cordifolia, a splendid
ground-cover plant
Botton left: The bedding dahlia Border Prince
Top right: Aquilegias, or Columbines
Bottom right: The pompon chrysanthemum Fairie

Top: Plantings of Michaelmas Daisies can bring welcome colour to the autumn garden
Bottom: The charming astilbes with their plume-like flowers and ferny foliage can be happily integrated in many planting schemes

plants must be moved in the spring and enjoy a taste of lime. They vary in height from 2–2½ ft. King George, deep purple; Lady Hindlip, deep rose; and Sonia, clear pink, are my choice from a large list.

Aster frikartii: a light blue, desirable plant being the first and last to flower (flowering from August to October), about 2½ ft. in height. This species must be propagated by division, the seed being infertile.

Aster novae-angliae: the *novae-angliae* group of asters has slightly rough, hairy leaves. The plants are tall and vigorous, growing to 4 ft. or more, but are unfortunately inclined to become bedraggled in bad weather. Varieties include Barr's Pink, 4–4½ ft., a rose-purple veteran that attracts the Red Admiral butterfly, and flowers in August and September; and Harrington's Pink, a delightful colour but a plant of poor habit, August to September flowering, 3½–4 ft. Both these close their flowers at night.

Aster novi-belgii: varieties of this species form a well-known group of single, semi- and fully double-flowered, smooth-leaved Michaelmas daisies, flowering from September onwards. They vary in height from 2½–5 ft.

There is an army of attractive plants in this group, due largely to the work of an enthusiastic hybridiser, the late Ernest Ballard of Colwall. Among the varieties he introduced are Apple Blossom, semi-double cream overlaid pink, 3–4½ ft.; Ernest Ballard, semi-double, rosy crimson, 3 ft.; Blandie, semi-double, creamy white and very popular, 3½–4 ft.; Eventide, violet-blue, 3 ft.; Winston S. Churchill, beetroot purple, 2½ ft.; and Lassie, a lovely shade of pure pink, with large flowers, 4 ft. This last variety has been given an Award of Merit by The Royal Horticultural Society.

The dwarf asters now come into the *novi-belgii* section. They are a grand race of pygmies, a mass of bloom, flowering madly through September and October. Varieties include Audrey, large pale blue flowers, 15 in.; Lilac Time, soft lilac, very free, even for a dwarf, 12 in.; Rosebud, soft pink, semi-double flowers, 15 in.; and Snowsprite, the best dwarf white variety, 15 in.

Aster yunnanensis Napsbury: this is a fine 1½-ft. purple-blue variety with an orange centre, raised at Napsbury Mental Hospital. It is a favourite for cutting. This plant demands a well-drained position and it has a tendency to lift itself out of the soil and should be refirmed when necessary. It should be divided and replanted every two or three years, directly after flowering or in the spring. Napsbury is undoubtedly one of the stars of the family.

I have attempted to give the gardener some idea of the vast scope of the modern Michaelmas daisy. Tall, of medium height, short or almost prostrate, it fulfils every purpose and has earned the title of 'maid-of-all-work' of the herbaceous border.

Propagation is by division in spring or autumn or by softwood cuttings rooted from March to June in a shaded frame of sandy soil.

Astilbe (False Goatsbeard). This herbaceous perennial is sometimes confused with the shrubby spiraea. The astilbes have charming plumes or panicles of cream, pink or red flowers which are borne in July and August (although some flower in June and July) and ferny foliage, sometimes mahogany tinted, in spring.

The astilbe is happy in borders when well mulched against dryness; it is at its happiest in moist soil by the waterside. Being an early developer it can be vulnerable to late frosts and if in a cold garden should be found a warm corner in semi-shade. The crowns should not be deeply planted and a mulch of well-decayed manure in the spring speeds growth and holds the moisture.

The *Astilbe arendsii* hybrids first raised by George Arends of Ronsdorf are an admirable group in many attractive colours and grow from 2½-5 ft. They include such varieties as Amethyst, lilac-purple; Bressingham Beauty, rich pink, and a long laster of perfect form; Ostrich Plume, clear pink, with arching sprays; Spinell, a striking fiery red, and White Queen.

There are a number of interesting astilbe species, among them being *A. astilboides,* 2–3 ft., with white flower spikes. *A. japonica* hybrids may be used for forcing in a cool house to provide early flowers.

Irises, primulas, artemisias, and Lamb's Ears (*Stachys lanata*) associate well with astilbes.

Propagation is by careful division of clumps in spring or autumn. Plants grown from seed seldom come true to type.

Balloon Flower, see Platycodon

Beard Tongue, see Penstemon

Bear's Breeches, see Acanthus

Bee Balm, see Monarda

Bellflower, see Campanula

Bergamot, see Monarda

Bergenia. The bergenias were formerly known as megaseas and before that as saxifragas. The bergenia is a useful plant with thick, cabbage-like leaves and spikes of pink or red flowers on rather clumsy stalks, arriving between February and May, depending on the species or variety. It is a magnificent ground-cover plant and is unfussy about soil or position. *Bergenia delavayi*, with reddish-purple flowers in March and April and red leaves in winter is a delightful species, but *B. cordifolia,* with round leathery leaves and spikes of dark pink flowers in April and May, is the species usually grown. There are white, pink-purple and bright pink-flowered varieties. *B. crassifolia aureo-marginata*, with variegated leaves and red flowers, in April, deserves to be seen more often. Height about 1 ft.

Propagation by division in autumn.

Betony, see Stachys

Bleeding Heart, see Dicentra

Brunnera. This plant used to be called *Anchusa myosotidiflora* and is still widely known under that name. With its forget-me-not-like flowers and large heart-shaped leaves this perennial is a charmer and makes an excellent ground cover. The May and June flowers are on 1½-ft. stems. This plant enjoys semi-shade, and may be propagated by seed sown in boxes in a cold frame in March.

The attractive Cranesbill *Geranium ibericum*, June–July flowering, with pyrethrums, Oriental Poppies and others. *Inset:* The single-flowered *Pyrethrum* Marjorie Robinson, which, like others of its genus, is a splendid variety for cutting

Bugle, see Ajuga
Bugloss, see Anchusa
Burning Bush, see Dictamnus
Buttercup, see Ranunculus
Button Snakeroot, see Liatris
Californian Tree Poppy, see Romneya
Campanula (Bellflower). This is a vast genus embracing a diversity of subjects distinguished by their bell-shaped flowers in blue, white and, occasionally, in pink.

Campanulas will grow in any good garden soil provided it is well drained. They have a taste for both lime and bonemeal and thrive in a sunny position, while managing in partial shade.

The family is long lived but vulnerable to rust, some varieties suffering more from the disease than others. Affected leaves should be burned and the plant treated with a copper dusting powder. Campanulas can be planted at any time between October and April, during suitable weather; being upright in habit, staking will seldom be found necessary.

Not all nurseries stock the named varieties; if one firm cannot supply the plants then another nursery should be tried. Listed below are a few of the many desirables:

Campanula carpatica: this is the Carpathian Bellflower which bears large, blue, bell-shaped flowers from June to September. Variable in habit, the varieties of the species are particularly useful in July–in between seasons–for the front of the border. They include Convexity, deep blue, 15 in.; Queen of Somerville, perhaps the best blue *carpatica*, 15 in.; and White Star, which has satiny white bells with stellate points, 12 in.

Campanula glomerata, the Danesblood, is a willing grower in almost all soils. It forms globular, terminal heads of rich violet flowers up to 2 ft. *C. g. superba* should be found a place, June–July flowering, 18 in., and *dahurica*, 1 ft.

Campanula lactiflora, the Milky Bellflower, is a splendid border plant with tall spikes of pale blue flowers borne on 5-ft. stems from June to August. Its variety Loddon Anna, 4–5 ft., a large and beautiful pink, has been given an Award of

Merit. Light blue Pouffe, 12–18 in., covers its leafy mounds with bloom for weeks on end from June to September.

Campanula latifolia, the Great Bellflower, is another stalwart species with stiff stems and large, pendant flowers. Its variety Brantwood with purplish-blue flowers on 4-ft. stems should not be missed. It will provide colour from June to August.

Campanula persicifolia, the Paper Bellflower, flowers in June and July and has blooms of fragile texture. Among its varieties are a number of fine named subjects flowering from May to July: *C. p. alba,* Fleur de Neige, double white; Telham Beauty, with rich blue flowers, and Wedgwood, a little paler than the rest. All are about 3 ft. in height.

Campanula portenschlagiana is a medium blue wonder plant for rock garden or wall, rather than the border. The sheets of bluish-purple flowers that arrive in May or June and continue into July entitle this species to head the list of the tufty and trailing campanulas that may mix happily in the foreground with the crocus species and the charming trickle of early spring flowers. Another attractive campanula for walls or banks in summer and early autumn is *C. poscharskyana,* with light blue flowers on 1-ft. stems and bright green foliage.

Now a word of warning about *C. rapunculoides,* a lightening-rooting gangster that can become a weed and menace. The fact that its roots are edible and can be served like parsnip cuts no ice with me.

Propagation is by seed or division of roots in spring or autumn, or from softwood cuttings in March.

Campion, see Lychnis

Candytuft, see Iberis

Cape Fuchsia, see Phygelius

Cape Gooseberry, see Physalis

Carnation, see Dianthus

Catananche (Cupid's Dart). This is a cornflower-type perennial with a zest for flowering for months on end. The foliage is hoary and grass-like, and the stems wiry; the flowers, dry and semi-everlasting, are of a papery quality.

This is a sun lover that prefers a light soil; if the soil is wet the bed should be raised and spring planting is advised. The catananche is not usually a long-lived plant and is apt to flower itself to death.

Catananche caerulea is a light cornflower blue; *C. c. major,* 2½ ft., the outstanding member of the family, should be the gardener's choice. It flowers from June to August. There are also both white and blue and white variegated forms.

Propagation is by seed in early spring, division in spring or root cuttings in autumn.

Catmint, see Nepeta

Centaurea (Knapweed). The flowers are of cornflower shape, varying in colour, some accompanied by attractive silver foliage. The Knapweed is strong growing and must be controlled, otherwise it will over-step its allotted space. Preferring a sunny position, it requires planting in ordinary good garden soil.

Centaurea dealbata, 2 ft., the Persian centaurea, has thistle-like rosy-magenta flowers. *C. macrocephala,* 3–4 ft., has large golden heads of bloom of interesting formation. *C. montana,* a real cornflower blue, is inclined to flop and straggle. *C. ruthenica,* 3 ft., with pretty straw-coloured heads, has branching stems and elegant dark green foliage.

Centaureas are not suitable plants for a very small garden and should be divided every two or three years.

Propagation is by division in spring or autumn.

Ceratostigma (Leadwort). This small perennial bears attractive periwinkle-like flowers in the late summer when the foliage turns a colourful plum red. It needs a warm position and sunshine. Considering its charms, it is not surprising that *C. plumbaginoides,* decked with dark blue flowers from July until the frost arrives, has become a great favourite. Height: anything from 9–18 in.

Propagation is by half-ripe cuttings in July or division in spring, preferably the first-mentioned.

Chalk Plant, see Gypsophila

Below: The white-flowered *Campanula latifolia alba*, an attractive variety of the Great Bellflower

Chamomile, see Anthemis

Cheiranthus (Wallflower). This plant, too well known to need description, is usually grown as a biennial (see p. 134), but there are a few truly perennial varieties well worth growing, flowering as they do so early in the season. Their scent is, of course, delicious.

The wallflower will only flourish on well-drained soil with perhaps a taste of lime and mortar rubble in its composition. As it is a member of the *Cruciferae* it suffers from the same pests and diseases as the brassicas. If both cabbages and wallflowers are grown, it is advisable to keep them apart to make sure that the troubles of one are not passed on to the other.

Cheiranthus Harpur Crewe, 9 in., the well-known woody, double yellow perennial wall-flower is my pick of the family. Other varieties are between 1–2 ft.

Propagation is by cuttings taken after flowering.

Chinese Bellflower, see Platycodon

Chinese Lantern, see Physalis

Chinese Trumpet Flower, see Incarvillea

Chrysanthemum. The hardy chrysanthemums are of great service to the autumn border and I should like to see them receive more attention. The 'early' florists' chrysanthemums which flower in August and have to be propagated every year in greenhouse or frame do not really look right in the border, and their large flowers suffer from rain and severe weather.

The Koreans and Rubellums are of main interest, for here are flowers that will come into bloom in late July and keep the beds and the house gay until the frost arrives.

The modern varieties are brighter than they were but there is still need for more sparkle, and scope for an enthusiastic hybridiser. Clear pinks, brilliant reds, creams and whites with tough constitutions are what we need, and less emphasis on the autumn shades.

A veteran gardener described the hardy group as 'Nature's chrysanths', the autumn answer to the busy gardener's prayer. Disbudding is not essential and there is little or no staking required. If open flowers are browned off by the frost, new

Top left: Campanula glomerata dahurica, a richly
coloured variety of the Danesblood
Bottom left: The bearded iris Snow Tracery
Top right: The striking *Geranium psilostemon*
Bottom right: The indispensable, winter-flowering
Iris unguicularis

44

buds will bloom unaffected. All that these willing plants ask for is a sunny position, a taste of well-rotted manure and bonemeal, and occasional feeds of liquid manure before flowering (and perhaps from time to time a sprinkling of lime, depending on the soil).

The daisy-like Korean chrysanthemums, $1\frac{1}{2}$–3 ft., come in pink, red, yellow, orange, bronze, cream and white. They have a bushy habit. The majority of the group are fully hardy but appreciate a sheltered position.

Bronze Tench, Copper Nob, and Purple Twinkle are favourites, but I prefer the pink shades such as Crimson Tench, rosy Janice Bailey, lilac-pink Melody and pastel Pa Dickson.

Rooted cuttings delivered in spring will make sturdy plants by the summer. There are several good strains of which the Otley group is outstanding. They flower from August onwards and there are single, semi-double and fully double hybrids: Gold Dust, yellow; Rosalie, pink; and Wedding Day, white, with a green centre and slightly fragrant. The last is a great favourite of mine but alas is rather tender.

The Cushion Koreans, dwarfs that form tiny hummocks that cover themselves with bloom, are most suitable for the windswept garden. Margery Daw, a single-flowered red variety, and Polly Peachum, double, rosy peach and often flowering for two months on end, are remarkably reliable.

The Rubellum chrysanthemums differ from the Koreans in rootstock formation. The Rubellums run underground like many of our most tiresome weeds. They are earlier than the Koreans, flowering from August onwards, and are considerably stouter in stamina with a proud record of having survived the arctic conditions of the 1946–1947 British winter. They come in all the usual chrysanthemum shades. Clara Curtis, $2\frac{1}{2}$ ft., a lovely clear pink, is the pride of the group.

Both the Koreans and the Rubellums are increased by division of plants in March, or by basal cuttings taken between mid-February and late March. These should be rooted singly in 2-in.

pots in a closed propagating case in a temperature of 10° to 16°C. (50° to 60°F.). They should then be grown on in a temperature of 7° to 13°C. (45° to 55°F.) and later either potted in individual $3\frac{1}{2}$-in. pots or boxes before being planted out in the garden.

Some mention should be made of the Sprays and formal Pompon chrysanthemums. Anyone interested in the poms should visit The Royal Horticultural Society's Garden at Wisley in the autumn where they present a magnificient display. The round heads and colourful rosettes of such brave small plants as the golden Denise, the purple Eve and the lilac Everley attract a host of admirers. The Koreans and Rubellums, Sprays and Pompons are best lifted for the winter and the stools cut back and boxed, then stored in a cold frame which can be given extra protection with matting in very cold weather.

Chrysanthemum maximum, the Shasta Daisy from the Pyrenees, is the familiar white daisy with a golden centre and another hardy chrysanthemum of note. Flowering in July and August at mid-season when few other varieties are in flower, it opens a new bud almost as soon as the flower arranger's scissors snip. A sun lover, it will grow almost anywhere provided the soil is not too dry. The well-known variety Mayfield Giant, $3\frac{1}{2}$ ft., has earned a good living for many a gardener in the past.

From *Chrysanthemum maximum* come a number of popular double white and cream hybrids, $2\frac{1}{2}$–3 ft., that are grown commercially by the acre; they are frequently dyed pink or yellow for the market. Among them are Esther Read, a large white flower but not an easy winter subject; Jennifer Read, a favourite with the florist, and Julischnee (July Snow) a first-class variety.

I end the chrysanthemum saga with a plant which deserves to be more seen, *C. uliginosum*, the Moon Daisy. Strong and bushy, it has single white, green-centred flowers as much as $2\frac{1}{2}$ in. across. This is an upstanding plant, $4\frac{1}{2}$–5 ft., for the back of the border, flowering in September and October.

Propagation is by division in autumn, and *C. maximum* varieties can also be increased by soft cuttings in mid-summer, grown on ready to fill the gaps caused by winter demises. Replanting should be undertaken every second year, immediately after flowering.

Chrysanthemum coccineum is the Pyrethrum, see p. 84.

Cinquefoil, see Potentilla

Clematis (Virgin's Bower). This genus is well known as a handsome, hardy climber, but it also includes some non-climbing border perennials worth growing.

A well-drained loam treated with a generous sprinkling of hydrated lime will suit these plants admirably. They also do well on chalky soils. They may be planted in spring or autumn and treated to a spring mulch of well-rotted manure.

Here are my pick of herbaceous varieties. *C. heracleaefolia davidiana* (Abbé David's Clematis) bears profuse clusters of scented, blue, hyacinth-like flowers from July to September. It produces strong shoots and large, rather coarse leaves. It grows up to 4 ft. *C. integrifolia*, 3–4 ft., has deep blue singly borne nodding flowers with white stamens in July. The leaves are oval and stalkless. There is also a white form of this species. *C. recta* is a species with panicles of sweetly scented, small, white flowers borne on strong stems in summer, 3 ft. The variety *flore pleno* bears delightful sprays of double flowers, and the variety *purpurea* has colourful purple-green leaves.

Propagation is by cuttings of young shoots rooted in a frame during the summer, or by division in autumn.

Columbine, see Aquilegia

Cone Flower, see Rudbeckia

Convallaria (Lily-of-the-Valley). The spring-flowering Lily-of-the-Valley (*Convallaria majalis*) needs no introduction. It enjoys a partially shady border and moist, rich soil to which well-rotted manure and leafmould has been added. Planting may be done in the autumn or spring, spreading out the roots carefully and covering them with about an inch of soil. The bed should be mulched

Top: The attractive *Crocosmia masonorum* which bears reddish-orange flowers in July and August
Bottom: The coreopsis are excellent dual-purpose flowers combining good garden qualities with suitability for cutting. Shown here is the large-flowered golden-yellow Perry's Variety

annually in February with decayed manure and the crowns replanted every four years.

Fortin's Giant is the best form, having good stamina and large flowers. The variety *rosea,* a rather disappointing pink, is a little overrated. The variegated form, *variegata,* will be appreciated by those who enjoy green- and white-foliaged plants, and the double Lily-of-the-Valley, the variety *prolificans,* will also have its admirers.

Propagation is by seed sown outdoors $\frac{1}{4}$ in. deep in a light soil in March, or by division of the crowns in September or October.

Coral Flower, see Heuchera

Coreopsis (Tick-seed). The large, flat, yellow flowers of the coreopsis are useful for cutting and are carried on slender stems throughout the summer. Ordinary soil and a sunny position suits these easy-going plants. They are long lived provided the soil is not over-rich.

Some of the best are: *C. auriculata,* golden-yellow with a maroon centre, June to September, 2 ft.; *C. grandiflora* Perry's Variety, semi-double, golden-yellow flowers from June to September, 2 ft., and the 3-ft. *C. g.* Badengold with bright semi-double golden-yellow flowers–but too shy flowering to please many–July to September, 3 ft.; *C. lanceolata,* with bright yellow flowers and large leaves, July to September, 2 ft., and the attractive, richly yellow *C. verticillata,* $1\frac{1}{2}$ ft.

Propagation is by seed (when results are likely to be variable) and by division in spring.

Cranesbill, see Geranium

Crocosmia. The small group of plants formerly known as montbretias are now called crocosmias. They consist of South African sun worshippers which do best in deep, sandy soil. The plants, which are grown from corms, are very showy with reddish-orange flowers on slender 1–$1\frac{1}{2}$-ft. stalks in late summer. The handsome *C. masonorum* is also a good plant for a warm border.

The plants should be lifted and divided every three years.

Cupid's Dart, see Catananche

Dahlia. The dahlia has an extensive colour range and is the most dazzling plant in the border from

An arrangement of delphiniums by Joan Dove. The chlorophytum, ivy, iris leaves and allium seed heads are a pleasing foil for the delphiniums

July until the frosts arrive. There is as yet no true blue variety, but Amethyst and Blue Mist belong to an army of hopefuls.

Dahlias are half-hardy and the tuberous roots should be lifted before the winter and returned to the garden in the late spring. These willing plants will grow in most gardens provided the soil is well dug to a depth of not less than 9 in. and enriched with well-decayed manure or compost. A light dressing of a balanced general fertiliser can be added to the surface soil when forking over the bed in the spring (3 to 4 oz. per sq. yd.) and an occasional application of liquid manure will be appreciated from July to September. Nitrogenous fertilisers, which lead to greenery rather than flowers, should be avoided.

Dahlias are gross feeders and drinkers and should be watered well and regularly in a really dry season. Mulching around the plants in early summer will reduce the chore of watering.

The tubers may be started into growth in pots in March or April in a temperature of about 13°C. (55°F.). It is usually safe to plant out during the third week of May, covering the tubers with 2 in. of soil to avoid the risk of young shoots being nipped by frost.

Young plants bought early in the season are apt to be fleshy and vulnerable to wind and low temperatures and such plants should be hardened off and planting delayed until the weather is kindly.

Correct spacing is important, the novice's besetting sin being to overcrowd. A few measurements may be helpful to the beginner. The large Decorative and Cactus varieties should be spaced 4 ft. apart. Smaller Decoratives and Cactuses, Collerettes, and the Paeony-flowered should be set about 3 ft. apart, and Dwarf Bedding varieties 18 in. apart. Staking is essential for all but the smallest kinds, using either bamboo or wooden stakes. If this is done when planting, the possibility of the tubers being injured is avoided.

If big individual blooms are desired rather than a large number of smaller ones, the young shoots should be limited to three in July and the flower buds reduced to one bud to each shoot in August.

Top growth will be blackened by the frost in the autumn. The plants should then be lifted and carefully stored in a frost-proof, airy place where there is sufficient moisture in the air to prevent the tubers from shrivelling. The airing cupboard will not do.

Dahlia tubers are prone to suffer from fungus trouble and rotting during the storing period. A precaution against this is to inspect the tubers at regular intervals, treating them with the fungicide thiram whenever necessary while they are in store.

There are ten classified groups of dahlias, ranging from the immense Giant Decoratives with blooms as much as $14\frac{1}{2}$ in. across to the Miniature Balls and Pompons, the singles and the lovely Collerettes with one or more rings of flattened ray florets. The last-mentioned are quite beautiful in their simplicity.

I cannot resist putting in a word for the small-flowered 'decs' that include the well-known shell pink Gerrie Hoek and lovely Vicky Crutchfield. These have the glamour of a water-lily and are perfect for cutting (although the showman may complain that the flowers are too flat and lacking in depth). The cactus dahlias, with fully double blooms and ray florets which are usually pointed, are perhaps the most popular of all. Also popular are the Dwarf Bedding kinds.

The dahlia has not only made tremendous strides in size, shape and colour during the last decade or two, but it has extended its flowering season. There are now dahlias that open their buds in late June.

A collection kindly chosen by Mr. John Crutchfield, the well-known dahlia specialist, is as follows:

Types	Varieties
Single (Dwarf Bedding)	Yellow Hammer
Anemone-flowered	Comet, crimson
Collerette	Sincerity, white
Peony-flowered	Bishop of Llandaff, red
Giant Decorative	Hamari Girl, Bengal rose

Right: The peony-flowered dahlia Bishop of Llandaff,
an established favourite with red flowers
Far right: The Giant Decorative Hamari Girl with
blooms of Bengal-rose colouring

Types	Varieties
Large Decorative	Mrs. McDonald Quill, red and white
Medium Decorative	Golden Turban, orange-yellow
Small Decorative	Gerrie Hoek, pink (for cutting)
Miniature Decorative	David Howard, orange (dark foliage)
Ball Dahlia	Rev. Colwyn Vale, purple
Miniature Ball	Cherida, salmon
Pompon	Willo's Violet
Giant Cactus	Polar Sight, white
Large Cactus	Superclass, dark pink
Medium Cactus	Curtain Raiser, orange
Small Cactus	Klankstad Kerkrade, yellow
Miniature Cactus	Romance, dark pink
Giant Semi-cactus	Croeso '69, pink and cream
Large Semi-cactus	Nantenan, yellow
Medium Semi-cactus	Autumn Fire, flame-yellow
Small Semi-cactus	Sonatine, bright yellow
Miniature Semi-cactus	Chalky, white

Propagation is by cuttings, division of the tubers or by seed. A packet of dwarf border mixed seed sown $\frac{1}{8}$ in. deep at the beginning of April will provide a host of medium-sized double and semi-double flowers, charming even if undistinguished. Professional growers propagate by cuttings and the division of tubers. The cuttings, 3-in. shoots arising from the tuber, should be put in 2-in. pots of sandy soil in a temperature of around 18°C. (65°F.) from February to the end of April. The tubers should be divided in the spring, each division with a small part of the main crown.

Day Lily, see Hemerocallis

Dead Nettle, see Lamium

Delphinium. This is the perennial larkspur, named after the dolphin, the unexpanded buds having reminded an ancient botanist of this spirited mammal.

The delphinium ranks high among border plants: the newcomers range in colour from palest sky blue to the darkest gentian, parma violet, heliotrope, mauves and shot mixtures of watered-silk quality, whites (with or without black eyes), pinks, and whether you like them or not, the much-discussed Strawberry Fair, and now on the verge of the market, a red.

The British blues are completely hardy, but the newer shades belonging to the Pacific strain may be found a trifle tender.

The flower spikes have a regal beauty but the less stately, with slimmer stems, that sway in the breeze, have recaptured the grace mislaid by some of the giants and broomstick monsters.

The modern tendency is towards the shorter and lighter stems that give with the wind and are more able to survive rough weather.

June and July are the peak flowering months for delphiniums, but if growth is cut back after the first flush of bloom there is always the hope that smaller spikes may appear to give a second performance towards the end of summer. However, this second flowering weakens the plants, and for this reason the expert usually limits himself to the first flowering and pinches out any buds which appear later.

Delphiniums relish a rich soil and it is vital that the top spit should be well dug in advance of planting and mixed with humus, leafmould, peat, spent hops, manure or garden compost. If the soil is light and sandy a generous amount of humus must be added and planting carried out in the autumn; if it is of clay or in other ways heavy, planting is best left until the spring.

The plants should be found a sunny, open position away from hedges or overhanging trees. Having dug a comfortably sized hole the crown should be planted just below the surface level in heavy soil and a few inches deeper when the soil is light.

A dressing of good general fertiliser in late April (3–4 oz. to each plant on medium and heavy soils, and 5–6 oz. on light) raked into the top inch of soil will be found rewarding. The plants should be watered copiously during May and June when the spikes are forming.

The gardener who wants quality and has his or her eye on the show bench must thin the flower spikes to two or three, while home growers should content themselves with five spikes. If the plants are allowed to bear a larger number of flowers a strain is put on the root system, which will inevitably tell the following season. Seedlings

or recently transplanted plants should not be allowed more than one flower head. The unwanted spikes should be cut off an inch or so above ground level as soon as they have declared themselves. A summer mulch will keep the plant roots cool and moist and will reduce the work of watering.

Supporting canes should be in position by the first week in May. To provide every flower spike with a cane is time consuming, and it will be found less laborious to place three canes round each plant in a triangle early in the season, linking these with string at intervals. This method allows the spikes to sway within the confines of the triangle and less damage is caused to the stems by wind than if individual canes were used for each spike. Four-foot tall supports should suffice for even the tallest varieties.

The flowers should be cut as they fade, so that the plant does not exhaust itself by seeding. In the autumn the nurseryman cuts down his delphiniums to 6–8 in. from the ground, leaving the stumps to indicate where the plants are stationed when they die down. The amateur grower may prefer to cut his plants down to ground level as they are unlikely to be quite as robust as those of the nurseryman, and there is the danger that water may collect in the hollow stems, resulting in rot.

The delphinium is a favourite springtime dish for all varieties of slugs and the common snail; a lusty slug can nibble the tips out of a box of seedlings overnight. The crowns should be protected with a covering of well-weathered ashes or sand and surrounded with strategically placed barriers of contact killers.

The Belladonna delphiniums have a delightful branching habit and are delicate and elegant. Two excellent varieties of this type are the pale blue Blue Bees and the deep blue and purple Wendy. *D. ruysii* (also known as Pink Sensation), a rather undecided pink, remains a favourite with some gardeners, and *D. zalil*, with pale yellow flowers borne on spindly spikes, attracts the gardener with a taste for the unusual.

The large-flowered hybrids of *D. elatum,* uncertain in lineage due to lost records, are the delphiniums so widely grown. In spite of the new colours and shades that have been introduced lately, the large-flowered blues remain firm favourites.

The gardener should look for a good 'holder', a variety that keeps its florets at the bottom of the stem fresh and intact until those at the top of the spikes have opened out. Good varieties include:

Colours	Varieties
Pale mauve	Bridesmaid, silvery mauve, and Silver Moon
Heliotrope	Cinderella, a heliotrope-mauve dwarf
Light blue	Cressida, pale sky blue with a white eye, and Lord Butler, pale Cambridge blue

Colours	Varieties
Dark blue	Fenella, gentian with a black eye, and Molly Buchanan, gentian blue, with a black eye
Dark purple and violet	Purple Triumph, violet-purple with a black and gold eye; Royal Marine, the finest purple; and Sabu, a violet self with a black eye, and the darkest delphinium we possess
White	Swan Lake, a superb flower with a contrasting black eye, and Icecap, a massive spike with blooms of pure white

I am flattered that Mr. Brian Langdon has named a lavender 1969 variety Xenia Field.

Delphiniums are increased by seed, cuttings or division. Seed is sown in March in pans of light soil in a temperature of 13°C. (55°F.) or outdoors in ½-in. deep drills in April, or by spring cuttings of young 3-in. shoots in pots of sandy soil placed in a cold frame. Seed from a home-grown spike can be sown in August and a packet of seed from a specialist is usually a happy speculation. Three of the best blues yet seen came out of a modestly priced packet of Bishop-strain seed. Roots are divided in September or March, each division including one or two strong shoots, a solid piece of healthy crown and a sound fibrous root system. Unrooted cuttings, taken in the spring, should be cut close to the ground to ensure a solid base and any wound dusted with charcoal. A cutting with a hollow stem is doomed from the start. A mixture of soil, sharp sand and peat, or vermiculite (soaked for eight hours before using) is a suitable rooting medium. Overwatering must be avoided, but cuttings should not be allowed to dry out.

Delphiniums dislike any form of heat and cuttings can be raised in a frame or box against a north wall, covering them over at dusk with sacking and waterproof. Rooted cuttings may be planted out in late May or June.

Dianthus (Carnations and Pinks). Devoted as I am to the entire dianthus family, the 'flower of the gods', space will only allow me to deal with a chosen few, the border carnations and the pinks.

Although the dianthus is comparatively easy to grow, it is, as a rule, short lived, and the gardener must be prepared to propagate annually, so that the young can take the place of the old, straggling and departed. Small, compact, and usually very fragrant, with decorative foliage, they are in and out of flower the summer through.

The border carnation is the grand member of the family. It is a hardy plant that can be grown successfully without pampering in an open position and well-drained soil. There are the Flakes and Bizarres (a Flake is a combination of two distinct colours; the Bizarre is of more than two), the Picotee (white or yellow with a narrow band of colour round the edge of each petal), the Fancies (speckled and flecked), and the Selfs (one colour throughout).

The Selfs are easy-going with the exception of the yellows and apricots that are apt to be temperamental. They should not be attempted until the gardener is on intimate terms with the family.

The border carnation enthusiast insists on a circular bloom with an immaculate contour. The carnation with a split calyx, however beautiful, should hang its guilty head. Only the pick of the varieties should be grown; as many as six layers or cuttings may be obtained from a good plant in one year.

Pot plants should be bought whenever possible. They will romp away without hesitation, putting their energy into a June or early July flowering. The dianthus demands a sunny position, open yet protected from draught. Good alkaline (acid-free) and well-drained soil, on the rich side, with an addition of mortar rubble, suits them well.

Border carnations refuse to grow in certain parts of England where the soil is hot and unappetising. Grit, lime and a taste of hop manure or well-rotted farm manure and a monthly dressing of old soot carefully hoed in from early April until the flowering season are appreciated.

A sprinkling of lime should be part of the spring routine. If the ground is soggy the bed is best raised. Roots should not be planted too deep. The plants should be kept 9 in. apart so that when established they can be increased by layering.

Carnations may be allowed to flower to their heart's content, but if large blooms are wanted the gardener must disbud to one a stem, not picking off too many buds at any one time, and treating the plants to a weekly dose of liquid manure. Light staking is usually necessary.

My favourite border carnation is clove-scented Merlin Clove, white with purple marks. I am also devoted to the scarlet Old Crimson Clove and its constant companion fancy Candy Clove.

Among easy and good looking selfs are the crimson Bookham Grand, the soft apricot Clunie, the white Eudoxia, the highly scented, crimson Gipsy Clove, the violet Imperial Clove and the yellow Sunray. Among the bright fancies the yellow, flaked-scarlet Catherine Glover, French grey and cerise Harmony and yellow, marked scarlet Thomas Lee are outstanding.

Propagation is by seed, cuttings, layers and division. As the dianthus is a short-lived plant, propagation is an important matter. I advise layering as probably the easiest way of increasing stock, in July or August. The plants can be layered even when in bloom if the 'grass' (carnation jargon for a shoot) is long enough to handle. An upward cut below a joint, half through the stem, is made, the stem then being pressed down into good sandy soil and securely pinned. Rooted layers can be severed from their parent in September.

The blooms of garden pinks usually possess a winning eye or dark central zone. The foliage, grey, blue-grey, grey-green and silver is unique. Some plants become quite blue with the spring, and all have the same friendly way of hugging the ground.

It is the show pink, an aristocrat with perpetual-flowering blood in its veins, that is to the fore, having a longer flowering season than the early summer border carnation.

The new show pink has a strong look of the Allwoodii type and the same nice bushy habit, but is taller and of perfect shape and colour. Like the carnation, it enjoys the sun and insists on a well-drained bed. It dislikes peat, has a taste for lime and positively revels in mortar rubble. Spring is the right time for planting. It greatly assists pinks to remove faded flowers regularly.

Of garden pinks Mrs. Sinkins, the white double with incomparable scent, now in her second century, is never forgotten, although White Ladies being a pure white of far superior form has surpassed her.

There are a host of delightful Allwoodii varieties but Doris, shrimp pink with a red eye, is a joy and must surely come first. White, crimson-eyed Alice, and single, pale shrimp pink, crimson-eyed Daphne are others that delight me. Of the laced pinks Laced Joy, London Poppet, Dad's Favourite–the double white, laced chocolate variety–and Prudence, pale pink and heavily purple laced are my choice.

Show pinks, almost as grand as the carnations, are the aristocrats of the group, and Show Beauty, deep pink with a maroon eye; Show Distinction, crimson-cerise and of particular merit; the vivid orange-scarlet Show Glory, striking in appearance and free flowering; and the pure white Show Pearl, are all perfect in form and colour.

Propagation is by seed, cuttings, layering, pipings–shoots pulled out of a joint–or division. The pinks should be replanted or divided in the autumn and not allowed to remain stationary for more than two seasons. Cuttings and pipings strike best in a cold frame in summer.

Hand-fertilised seed obtained from a dianthus specialist and sown in sandy soil in January or February in a warm greenhouse or in a cold frame in the spring will give a good return.

Dicentra (Bleeding Heart). This is the graceful Dielytra, Bleeding Heart, Lyre Flower, Lady-in-the-Bath or Dutchman's Breeches, with arching stems festooned with locket-shaped flowers in May and June.

The foliage of *Dicentra spectabilis*, $1\frac{1}{2}$–2 ft., is fern-like, decorative and pale green. This beautiful and obliging perennial I have found content to grow at the foot of a north wall or even in a shaded corner where other plants may have failed to flower.

An ordinary light rich soil suits this plant, but good drainage is essential. Indeed, it has the reputation of being a little tender, resenting wet winter conditions. For this reason, some Dutch growers lift their plants in the autumn and box them up like dahlias. Left in the ground, the plants' crowns can be protected during the winter with a covering of ashes or old manure. If the gardener interplants with Solomon's Seal, iris or pyrethrums, the dicentra will be helpfully protected against cold spring winds.

During a hot summer or period of drought, the foliage is apt to die back and dust-dry corners of the garden should be avoided when planting. If the plants are cut down to ground level after flowering an autumn crop of bloom is encouraged.

Dicentra spectabilis makes a satisfactory and handsome pot plant if dug up and planted in a 7-in. pot in November. Placed in a frame or slightly heated greenhouse it will give a welcome early spring performance. The temperature should not be allowed to rise above 16°C. (60°F.), otherwise the rosy-pink and white flowers will be robbed of their colour. After flowering the plant may go back to the border.

The Dutchman's Breeches is an enduring long-lived subject that deserves a place in every garden where congenial conditions can be provided.

Dicentra eximia, 1 ft., has small carmine flowers which are borne in drooping racemes from May to August. It has attractive grey-green foliage. The variety *alba* has white pendulous flowers and finely cut foliage. Another decorative dicentra is *D. formosa* Bountiful, 12–15 in., a pink-red hybrid from America with a long flowering season and slightly glaucous foliage. But *D. spectabilis*, the real Bleeding Heart or Lady-in-the-Bath, is the most desirable member of the family.

Increase is by division, either when the plants are resting from October onwards or in early spring. The fleshy rootstock may be divided in the same way as dahlias, care being taken to ensure that each portion of root possesses at least one eye or bud. Plants can also be increased by

Top: An Allwoodii laced pink. The beautiful markings of this type give the blooms a delicacy which adds to their charm
Bottom: The graceful Bleeding Heart,
Dicentra spectabilis, with rosy-pink and white flowers

means of root cuttings taken in March or April and grown on in a cold frame.

Dictamnus (Burning Bush or Gas Plant). *Dictamnus albus* has tall (2-ft.) spikes of decorative white or pink flowers with long stamens. On a hot, windless day a match held close to the flower spikes will ignite the plant's volatile oil secretion. An easy doer, it prefers a light soil and plenty of sun.

The flowers may be lilac or pure white in colour and are borne in June and July.

Propagation is by seed sown in August or September, by cuttings of fleshy roots inserted 2 in. deep in a frame in March or April, or by division of the roots in October, November or March.

Doronicum (Leopard's Bane). This plant with a yellow daisy flower makes a dashing splash of colour in April and gives the border a first taste of summer. Unfussy about soil and willing to grow in semi-shade, this plant is invaluable. *D. plantagineum excelsum* (syn. Harpur Crewe), $2\frac{1}{2}$–3 ft., with flowers–excellent for cutting–as much as 3 in. across in April, May and June; the dwarf Miss Mason, $1\frac{1}{2}$ ft., with pale yellow flowers in April and May; and another dwarf Spring Beauty, $1\frac{1}{2}$ ft., with double, dark yellow flowers in May and June, are good garden forms.

Propagation is by division of the roots in October or March.

Echinacea. *Echinacea purpurea* is known in some parts of the country as the Hedgehog Flower and is closely related to the rudbeckia. A stately plant of 3–4 ft., even if a trifle coarse, it bears handsome, wide-rayed, purple-red daisy flowers in summer. It dislikes disturbance and should be left alone whenever possible. *E. purpurea* Robert Bloom, carmine-purple with an orange centre, and the reddish-purple, black-centred The King are both valuable acquisitions.

Propagation is by seed sown outdoors in April; by division in October, March or April, or by root cuttings taken in October.

Echinops (Globe Thistle). The globular flower heads of the echinops, perfect spheres of tightly

Top: *Dictamnus albus,* the Burning Bush
Bottom: The eremuri or Foxtail Lilies are among the
most handsome of border flowers and deserve a
commanding position in the garden

packed blue flowers, and the prickly foliage, make
these plants of real garden value. The flowers are
followed by metallic-blue spiky seed heads.
Hardy and easy to grow, the Globe Thistle
should be given an open position and ordinary
good soil.

Echinops humilis Taplow Blue is a grand plant
of about 5 ft. in height with dark blue globes,
and *E. ritro,* 4 ft., with steel-blue flowers, is my
second choice. Both flower in July and August.

Propagation is by seed sown outdoors in April;
by division of the roots between October and
March, or by root cuttings taken in late autumn
or winter and raised in a cold frame.

Eremurus (Foxtail Lily). The eremuri are
extremely handsome, with strong spikes of starry
flowers. The crowns of the plants are slightly
tender and, being vulnerable in spring to damp
and frost, benefit by a protection of dry litter
and a sprinkling of sand; the roots should be
given a covering of at least 6 in. The Foxtail Lily
does well on chalky soil.

There are a number of species and hybrids: the
bright yellow June-flowering *E. bungei,* 2–3 ft.;
E. elwesii, with lovely long spikes of soft pink
flowers in May and June, 8 ft.; *E. olgae,* with
starry, white, striped brown flowers in July, 4 ft.;
and *E. robustus,* pink and flowering in May and
June, the giant of the family, 9–10 ft. The
Shelford hybrids, 6 ft., are attractive plants with
flowers of orange, buff and pink in June and July.

Propagation is by seed, sown in a frame in a
sandy soil as soon as gathered, or by division in
autumn.

Erigeron (Fleabane). This is a useful genus
because of its long flowering season from May to
September. Not unlike the aster in form, it is
earlier to flower and shorter in stature, seldom
requiring support. It is an easy plant to please,
enjoying an open position and ordinary good soil.

There is a long list of erigeron hybrids of uncertain origin, among them mauve-blue Dignity;
deep pink Gaiety, excellent for cutting; White
Quakeress, and the erect pink Vanity – average
height 2½ ft. *E. mucronatus* is an elegant miniature

Top: The erigerons, with aster-like flowers, are easy to please
Bottom: The semi-shrubby *Euphorbia wulfenii* is a decorative plant in spring with its heads of close-packed green-yellow flowers

(only 9 in.), white tinted rose in colour. It is a happy and rampant wall plant and flowers for most of the summer.

Propagation is by seeds sown in spring or by division of the clumps in spring or autumn.

Eryngium (Sea Holly). The eryngiums are interesting and statuesque plants with stiff, jagged leaves and steel-blue flowers in late summer that are well worth drying for winter decoration. The plants do best in a light, sandy soil and are likely to disappear if the ground is at all waterlogged. There are a number of diverse species, the large-leaved ones being slightly tender.

Eryngium agavifolium, 5–6 ft., bears green-white flowers on branching stems. The dwarfs such as deep violet Jewel and the intense dark blue Violetta, both 3 ft., should also be considered.

Propagation is by seed sown in boxes in sandy soil in a frame during April or May; division in autumn or spring, or by root cuttings in autumn or winter in a cold frame.

Erysimum. The erysimums are near relatives of the wallflowers (see p. 134), and the species grown are quite small plants suited to the rock garden or the front of the border. A special favourite of mine is the 9-in. *Erysimum alpinum* Moonlight, with pale yellow flowers from May onwards through the summer.

Propagation is by seeds sown in June or by cuttings in summer in a frame.

Euphorbia (Milkweed, Spurge). The flowers are often inconspicuous but the bracts are interesting. These plants have found favour during the past decade. An ordinary, rather dry soil and a sunny position suits the spurges well. They are best planted in the spring.

I admire *E. ephithymoides (E. polychroma)* with sulphur-coloured spring flowers that form bright yellow, green-tinted clumps of about $1\frac{1}{2}$ ft. and the noble 3–4-ft. semi-shrub *E. wulfenii*—recently renamed *E. veneta*—with bottle-brush-like growth on long stems that bear large heads of small green-yellow flowers through the spring. These are wonderful plants for those who appreciate fine foliage in green-yellow and bluish-green shades.

Top: The white spikes of the Spire Lily,
Galtonia candicans, which appear in late summer
Bottom: The dwarf fuchsia Tom Thumb is a plant well
suited for the front of a mixed border

Propagation is by seed sown in a dryish spot in April or by division of plants in October or April.

Evening Primrose, see Oenothera

Everlasting Flower, see Helichrysum

Fair Maids of France, see Ranunculus

False Goatsbeard, see Astilbe

Flax, see Linum

Fleabane, see Erigeron

Foam Flower, see Tiarella

Foxtail Lily, see Eremurus

Fuchsia. This deciduous shrub often finds its way into the modern mixed border. There are the semi-hardy varieties that survive in Cornwall, Devon and on the west coast of Scotland and Ireland and a small number that thrive in any reasonably warm part of England and Wales, provided they are given winter protection in the form of bracken, leaves or sacking. A covering of 6 in. of weathered ash at the base of the plant is advised in cold parts of the country. The previous season's growth should be left unpruned until February or March when the protective material may be removed and all growth pruned back almost to ground level.

Fuchsias thrive in a good loam soil with leaf-mould and a sprinkling of sand worked in. They should be found a slightly shady position.

Fuchsia magellanica gracilis variegata will please the gardener looking for grey-white and silvery foliage suffused with red. This variety makes a bush of some 3 ft. *F. magellanica riccartonii*, 6–8 ft., with purple and red flowers that give a display from July to October, is a graceful member of the hardy group; Madame Cornelissen, scarlet and white, 2½–3 ft.; Mrs. Popple, with large flowers in scarlet and deep violet, 4 ft., and the dwarf Tom Thumb, cerise and mauve, 1½–2 ft., are all reliable garden plants.

Propagation is by cuttings taken in June, July or August and rooted in a frame.

Galtonia (Spire Lily). The giant white *Galtonia candicans* (syn. *Hyacinthus candicans*) is the bulbous plant so often seen in the summer border that it is fair to include it here. The flowers appear in late summer and are borne on 4-ft. stems. It requires a

good soil and plenty of sun, the bulbs being lifted and replanted when they show signs of becoming overcrowded.

Propagation is by seed sown in shallow boxes of sandy soil in a frame in the spring or autumn, or by offsets.

Gas Plant, see Dictamnus

Gentiana (Gentian). This is the most brilliant blue flower of them all.

Gentians enjoy a soil which includes peat and leafmould in its make-up, that does not dry out in the summer or become too wet in winter. They are hardy but resent heavy rainfall and changeable weather. Some of the mountain species are happier grown in a pan in a cool greenhouse than in the border. The plants can be helped through their first season by giving them the protection of a sheet of glass or cloche. A light topdressing of leafmould and peat will be enjoyed after flowering.

Different growers offer different advice on this rather temperamental plant, but nearly all agree that it is dangerous to allow the plant's roots to become parched in summer and that certain kinds resent the slightest suspicion of lime. *Gentiana acaulis*, 3 in., which provides a fanfare of large, blue trumpets in spring, and *G. sino-ornata*, 4 in., which bears its deep blue flowers in autumn (and has a strong dislike of lime), are two lovely, comparatively easily grown species although the former can be temperamental. *G. verna*, 2–3 in., a vivid deep blue spring flowerer which not only tolerates lime but actually appears to enjoy it, is a good beginner's plant, as is *G. septemfida*, 6–8 in., with clusters of deep blue flowers in summer. *G. asclepiadea*, the Willow Gentian, with arching 1½–2-ft. stems and rich pure blue flowers at their tips in July and August, is a willing grower if given a moist situation and partial shade. The white-flowered *G. a. alba* has particular charm.

Propagation is by seed sown in pans of sandy soil in a frame or greenhouse in March, or by division in the spring.

Geranium (Cranesbill). This is the true geranium and a hardy perennial (the plants commonly and incorrectly known as geraniums are pelargoniums).

Top: One of the geum hybrids which flower
from May to August
Bottom: Heleniums are undemanding plants which bring
welcome colour to the border in the latter half of
summer. The bronze-yellow variety Wyndley is shown
here

The Cranesbill has the charm and the look of a wild flower. The fashion for woodland and informal gardens, and for ground-cover plants, has now brought this somewhat neglected genus to the fore. Geraniums are willing growers in ordinary good soil in either partial shade or sun.

There are a large number of species, among them the striking magenta-red *Geranium psilostemon* (syn. *G. armenum*), 2½ ft., and the deep purple *G. phaeum*, 2 ft., both of which are May–June flowering and must be carefully sited so that they do not clash with their neighbours. *G. ibericum*, with purple-blue flowers carried on 1½-ft. stems in June and July, is another desirable species. *G. endressii*, 1 ft., with cup-shaped pink flowers, and its varieties, the bright rose Wargrave, 1½ ft., and the silver-pink A. T. Johnson, are a trio that bloom throughout the summer.

Geranium pratense, the blue Meadow Cranesbill, with wide open, blue, saucer-like flowers, is still to be found growing wild in certain parts of the country. The single and double blue and the white varieties of this species deserve to be grown. *G. sanguineum*, the Bloody Cranesbill, is a brilliant magenta-coloured species that makes a telling splash of colour in the front of the border. So much for a few of the many.

Propagation is by seed (under glass in early March or out of doors in late March or April) and root division in spring and autumn.

Geum. Easy to grow and bright in colour, the geum hybrids have a part to play in the majority of herbaceous borders. It is generally believed that *Geum chiloense* is the parent of the garden hybrids grown. Lady Stratheden, a clear yellow with semi-double flowers from May to August, and semi-double, scarlet Mrs. Bradshaw are grand old standbys; the flame-coloured Fire Opal (May to July) and Prince of Orange (June to August) are also good plants. The foliage forms neatly shaped rosettes, and the plants grow to a height of 1–2 ft.

The 1-ft. *G. borisii* is recommended for the front of the border. The single flowers are tangerine-scarlet and the plant is seldom caught

60

Top left: *Lychnis chalcedonica*, the Maltese or Jerusalem Cross
Bottom left: The helianthemums or Sun Roses are splendid free-flowering evergreen sub-shrubs for a sunny border

Top right: Nepeta, the well-known Catmint, provides colour through the summer
Bottom right: *Kniphofia* Royal Standard, a popular Red-hot poker

Top: The elegant *Gypsophila paniculata* Bristol Fairy
Centre: The splendid *Helianthus decapitalus* Loddon Gold
with golden-yellow flowers from August to October
Bottom: The Christmas Rose, *Helleborus niger*

out of bloom from June to September. Geums are content in ordinary good soil and should be given an open, sunny position.

Propagation is by seed sown in March in a cool greenhouse or frame, and division in spring or autumn.

Globe Flower, see Trollius

Globe Thistle, see Echinops

Gold Dust, see Alyssum

Golden Marguerite, see Anthemis

Golden Rod, see Solidago

Gromwell, see Lithospermum

Gypsophila (Chalk Plant). The slim grey stems smothered with a cloud of small flowers gives this plant a fairy-like appearance in summer. It grows into a rounded bush and is splendid for cutting. As its common name indicates, it is a lime and mortar rubble lover, but it is unfussy about soil so long as its hungry tap root can dive deep in search of good fare.

Gypsophila paniculata, or Baby's Breath, with grass-like leaves and masses of minute white or pink single flowers in loose panicles in summer, has gossamer charm and is longer lived than the doubles. It is about 3 ft. tall.

Bristol Fairy, 4 ft., is extremely elegant, while Rosy Veil, a semi-prostrate, double variety of only 9 in., has flowers that start white and turn pink. Flamingo, 3 ft., another pink variety with double flowers, given a tremendous boost on its introduction, is, in my experience, a little disappointing.

Propagation is not easy, but robust basal side-shoots with a heel taken in summer should root in sand if kept close and moist.

Helenium (Sneezeweed). This is another daisy-like family in all shades of mahogany, chestnut red, bronze and yellow. The heleniums are contented, undemanding plants provided the soil is not too sun baked and dry. There is a long list of garden varieties, many the progeny of *H. autumnale*. Moerheim Beauty, 3 ft., a large rich crimson variety, is still the best of these. Of the rest, bright yellow The Bishop, 3 ft., is outstanding. The heleniums flower in the latter half of summer.

Top: The graceful heucheras, or Coral Bells,
include the desirable modern introduction
Bressingham Blaze shown here
Bottom: Hydrangea paniculata grandiflora, a striking
shrub which can be grown successfully in the company of
perennials and other plants

Propagation is by seed sown in a cool green-house in spring, or by division in spring and autumn.

Helianthemum (Sun Rose). The helianthemum is closely related to the cistus, or rock rose, and demands plenty of sun and a light, sandy, well-drained soil.

The varieties of the evergreen sub-shrub *Helianthemum nummularium* provide delightful splashes of colour in the summer border, their colours including crimson, orange, pink, yellow and white. Of the many single and double varieties available, I would specially mention the semi-double, pink, orange-centred Rose Queen and The Bride, a white variety with grey foliage. The growth is inclined to flop after flowering has finished, when it should be cut back, using shears if the wood is tough.

There are a large number of varieties, both single and double, in crimson, orange, pink, yellow and white.

The species *H. tuberaria,* 1 ft., is a trailing perennial plant which bears spikes of yellow flowers in June and July.

Propagation can be by seed, but varieties are best raised by cuttings of half-ripe shoots inserted in sandy soil in a cold frame in August or September.

Helianthus (Sunflower). The helianthus is one of the tallest of the herbaceous border's residents and the flowers are in different shades of yellow. Its vigorous underground roots are invasive and need control. Stems may be cut down in October. The plants should be watered in drought and fed with a stimulant if the gardener is interested in height and size.

The variety most often seen is *Helianthus decapetalus* Loddon Gold, a fine, glowing double yellow flowering from August to October, often reaching 6 ft. *H. atrorubens* Monarch, 6–7 ft., with an almost black centre and rough foliage, is magnificent but slightly tender. If disbudded, it presents immense flowers 6–8 in. in diameter in September and October. Some gardeners lift the plants in the late autumn, placing them in a cold frame until the spring, and find it worth while.

Right: The outstanding herbaceous peony
Lady Alexandra Duff
Below: Lilium auratum, the Golden-rayed Lily of Japan

Propagation is by seed sown outdoors in April, or division of the roots in autumn or spring.

Helichrysum (Everlasting Flower). This is a widely differing genus with only a few perennial species. The bracts are dry and hard and keep their colour for long periods. Helichrysums are sun lovers which thrive on poor soil but are unable to stand up to wet and cold conditions.

Helichrysum plicatum, $3\frac{1}{2}$ ft., is often grown for its silver foliage, but the yellow flowers are insignificant. *H. virginicum,* only 6 in., with soft flat grey-green hummocks and panicles of primrose flowers of papery quality, is an attractive plant for a warm sunny spot.

Propagation is by seed sown out of doors in April or by cuttings rooted in a cold frame in spring.

Hellebore, see Helleborus

Helleborus (Hellebore). The Christmas Rose *(Helleborus niger)*, in white, is a long-lasting early flowerer that, once established, should be left undisturbed. It likes a shady well-drained position, a rich loam and a mulch with well-decayed

64

manure in April. An occasional feed of liquid manure during the summer will improve the plant's performance.

Helleborus corsicus, 2–3 ft., with clusters of pale apple-green flowers in February and March and glaucous green foliage, is a striking plant. *H. foetidus* (the Stinking Hellebore), 2 ft., has light green flowers and dark, distinguished, upright foliage and thrives in the shade. *H. niger,* 1 ft., the best known of the family, has pure white saucer-like flowers with golden anthers and deep green leaves but the flowers, unfortunately, are short stalked. It is possibly the easiest to grow.

Helleborus orientalis is the Lenten Rose of Greece and Asia Minor that has been followed by a number of desirable hybrids in cream, pink, purple, plum and black, either plain or spotted, $1\frac{1}{2}$–2 ft. These flower from January to March.

Propagation is by seeds sown $\frac{1}{8}$ in. deep in shallow boxes of sandy soil in a cold frame in October or March, planting out the resulting plants when they are about nine months old; or by division of roots in March.

Hemerocallis (Day Lily). The lily-like, trumpet blooms of the new American hybrids in shades of red, orange, pink, yellow and apricot are quite beautiful. Two or three flowers are carried on one stiff stem and the foliage is narrow and rush-like. Each flower lasts but one day so that the day lily makes a quiet appeal rather than a colourful splash, but a succession of flowers is produced over several months in summer.

Hemerocallis thrive in ordinary soil, preferring the moist to the dry, and are happy in sun or partial shade. Large clumps should be divided when the flowers show signs of deterioration.

The 3-ft. *H. fulva* with orange-brown flowers is one of the more interesting species, but it is the garden hybrids that have taken the gardener by storm – varieties such as Apricot, a glorious chrome yellow, and Black Prince, a ruby purple. Mostly around 3 ft. but ranging from 1–4 ft., they flower from June to August or September. These newcomers are a revelation and they are rapidly increasing in number.

Propagation is by division of the roots in October or March.

Heuchera (Alum-root, Coral Flower). This is a much-improved plant due to the work of enthusiastic hybridisers. The graceful sprays carrying small bell-shaped flowers are to be had in pink, carmine, copper and crimson. This attractive plant responds to good treatment and an annual mulch of well-rotted manure. Ordinary good, well-drained soil is suitable; clay soil may prove too wet for this plant.

Heuchera sanguinea is the most popular species. The scarlet Huntsman, 2 ft., and the off-white Pearl Drops, 2 ft., are splendid varieties. The Bressingham Hybrids, 1–2 ft., in pinks and reds are excellent value for the border and cutting.

A new race of plants known as heucherellas has been introduced by crossing heuchera varieties with *Tiarella cordifolia*. Bridget Bloom, a light pink variety of 18 in. is a delightful introduction that does best in light soil and partial shade.

Propagation is by division in spring.

Himalayan Poppy, see Meconopsis

Hosta (Plantain Lily). This splendid foliage plant was once known as Funkia. The noble leaves are in different shades of green or variegated; the tubular flowers are on loose spikes in subdued lilac or white. This is an indestructible plant that has become one of the leading ground-cover subjects.

Hostas appear to adapt themselves to any soil but prefer the moist and acid, with an addition of old rotted manure, peat or compost. Willing to grow in sun or shade, the leaves are larger when the plants are grown in shade, but the flowers are less exuberant. There are some thirty or forty species for the collector to choose from. I give but a few of my favourites.

Hosta crispula, $1\frac{1}{2}$ ft., is especially attractive with long, undulating leaves of rich green with a wide white margin. It bears lavender flowers in August. *H. fortunei,* 2 ft., with broad sage-green leaves, is easy to satisfy and makes excellent ground-cover. The pale mauve flowers appear in July. *H. f. albopicta,* $1\frac{1}{2}$ ft., is a gem in spring with

Top: The Day Lilies, hemerocallis, are handsome plants with a quiet appeal
Bottom: Hosta crispula, a Plantain Lily with white-margined, undulating leaves

butter-yellow leaf blades edged with light green. *H. sieboldiana* (syn. *H. glauca*) is the blue-green-leaved species with grand heart-shaped leaves that are deeply ribbed, and mauve flowers in June. *H. undulata,* 15 in. or so, has very wavy almost twisted foliage of a rich green, splashed centrally with creamy white, and pale lilac flowers in August.

Propagation is by division in spring or autumn.

Houseleek, see Sempervivum

Hydrangea. This is a summer-flowering shrub that on occasion makes its way into the mixed border. The flowers vary in colour, depending both on their variety and the content of the soil (usually in pink and red when on lime and blue when on peat or acid land).

Hydrangeas enjoy sun or partial shade, but being slightly tender they are best left unpruned until the spring so that any die-back caused by hard weather can be removed at that time. The flowers may also be left as a protection for the following year's buds. The plants should be protected with a light covering of sacking or bracken if the winter is severe. In March or April they may be cut down to within 1 in. of the base.

The varieties grouped under the name *Hydrangea macrophylla hortensia* are not completely hardy, although once established they are often capable of holding their own in the garden. They have large round flower heads in blue, pink and white. They usually grow to 6 ft. or rather more in height. *H. paniculata grandiflora,* 6 ft. tall, is one of more hardy species and its lovely creamy heads are a great feature in July and August.

Propagation is by cuttings of young shoots, inserted in sandy soil under a bell glass in heat in spring, or in a cold frame in August, or by suckers from the parent plant in spring or autumn.

Iberis (Candytuft). This is a bushy evergreen sub-shrub with masses of white flowers in May. A sun lover, it is inclined to trespass and should be cut back after flowering.

Iberis sempervirens Snowflake, trimmed hard after flowering, makes a gay dwarf shrub of about 1 ft. and Little Gem, only 6 in., is an even more

Left: Oriental Poppies, varieties of *Papaver orientale*, are a spectacular sight in May and June
Below right: *Rudbeckia sullivantii* Goldsturm, a splendid variety for August–September colour

generous flowerer and the best known of the family.

Propagation is by seed or summer cuttings rooted in a frame.

Incarvillea (Chinese Trumpet Flower). Rosy-red trumpets in fuchsia shades and pinnate deeply cut leaves characterise this plant. It is a plant that gives a good account of itself in light, sandy soil with a taste of well-rotted manure.

Incarvillea delavayi, with bright rich rosy-red flowers on 2-ft. stems in June and July, is handsome. The softer-coloured *I. grandiflora* Bees' Pink, 1 ft. and flowering in May-June, has many admirers.

Propagation is by seed or careful division of the tuberous roots in spring.

Inula. This is another yellow, daisy-shaped flower suitable for the informal border. It is unfussy, provided the soil is not too acid. *Inula orientalis,* 2 ft., the orange-yellow Caucasian species with ragged petals, is distinguished and a good flower for cutting.

Propagation is by seed (apt to be variable) or division in autumn or spring.

Iris. The tall bearded irises which bring such beauty to the garden in May and June have been greatly improved by the hybridisers over the last decade. Colours are brighter, the substance is tougher and the broad petals have ruffles or neatly tailored waves according to taste. Particularly striking are the new pink introductions. The iris specialist is proud that the falls have fewer half-markings (known as striation).

Irises are hardy and suitable for almost every garden. Heavy clay can be lightened by the introduction of old brick and mortar rubble and the addition of coarse sand or compost.

A topdressing of superphosphate of lime in April is helpful, using 1–2 oz. to each sq. yd. (builder's lime should be avoided) and a sprinkling of bonemeal, for the iris has a healthy appetite. Stable manure, if used, must be well rotted.

The rhizomes need sunshine and their performance the following summer is all the better for a thorough baking. The creeping potato-like rhizome should be three-quarters submerged in the soil, and lie like a turtle in the water.

I like to see irises planted in drifts in raised borders and can recommend tall white irises as pleasing company for apricot lupins. There is a flood of attractive varieties and in the brief selection below I have tried to illustrate the wide range of colours.

White: White City, with a flush of blue; Wabash, white, with violet falls. Pale blue: Horizon. Mid-blue: Jane Phillips, lightly ruffled and an unbeatable veteran. Deep blue: Blue Ensign, perfect shape. Black: Egyptian Night. Golden-yellow: Ola Kala. Café au lait: Jean Cayeux. Copper: Bryce Canyon. Chocolate brown: Louvois. Pink: Loomis V20. Pink (salmon): Strathmore, the Queen Mother's choice. Pink (orchid): Dreamcastle, with a near-white beard. Red: Quechee. Purple: Vice Regal. The tall bearded iris has a height range of $2\frac{1}{2}$–$4\frac{1}{2}$ ft., most varieties being about 3 ft. tall.

Something must be said about the April and May-flowering dwarf iris such as *I. pumila* that

Top: Fragrant lavender, a dwarf shrub which blends well with many garden features
Bottom: The lovely white-flowered *Lilium candidum*

grows from 5–12 in. Blue Pygmy, only 9 in., is a gem, and these thoughts on irises cannot be concluded without a word about *I. unguicularis* (once known as *I. stylosa*), growing to 1 ft., that flowers intermittently through the winter if grown against a south wall. This indispensable plant with slim, pencil-shaped buds opens its lilac-blue flowers along with the yellow winter jasmine (*Jasminum nudiflorum*) and the white winter-flowering cherry (*Prunus subhirtella autumnalis*), and with a sprig of Witch Hazel (*Hamamelis mollis*) makes an ideal vase for the mantelpiece. *I. unguicularis* likes a gritty, impoverished soil and can be planted after flowering or in the autumn.

The bearded irises are fast growers and can be increased by division of the rhizomes every second or third year, immediately after flowering, or by off-sets in the autumn.

Jacob's Ladder, see Polemonium

Kansas Gay Feather, see Liatris

Kentranthus (Red Valerian). I am devoted to this grand dry-wall plant that grows wild in many parts of the country. The main flush of rosy-pink flowers arrives in June but the plant throws up occasional spikes of bloom throughout the summer. It is also known under the name Centranthus.

Content with the poorest of soils the Valerian demands a sunny position and good drainage. The wild pink and white forms are outshone by the tall, rich deep crimson *K. ruber coccineus,* 3 ft., with glossy green leaves. There can be no more trouble-free plant than the Red Valerian.

Propagation is easy from seed sown in a frame or greenhouse in March, but choice kinds should be increased from cuttings. Self-sown seedlings can be a nuisance.

Knapweed, see Centaurea

Kniphofia (Red-hot Poker, Torch Lily). The kniphofia is a tropical-looking plant of character, with scarlet, orange, yellow and white varieties, and grass-like tufts of foliage. They are hardy but with a dislike of cold, wet soil. Protection should be given by tying the foliage together round the crowns in the late autumn.

70

There are a number of striking kinds, among them flame-red *Kniphofia erecta,* with upturned tubes, which makes its display in late summer and autumn. This particular hybrid is slightly tender and temperamental, but very well worth cultivating. *K. uvaria,* with orange-scarlet and yellow flowers in July and August, is the true Red-hot Poker, and *K. u. grandiflora* is a reliable orange-red in colour.

There are hybrids galore that come and go but the straw-to-white-coloured Maid of Orleans is an outstanding American variety that holds its place and gives a fine display which continues into autumn. The scarlet and gold Royal Standard is a firm favourite.

Propagation is by seed or division in spring or autumn.

Knotweed, see Polygonum
Lady's Mantle, see Alchemilla
Lamb's Ears, see Stachys
Lamium (Dead Nettle). Lamium is a prostrate ground-cover plant that will make itself at home almost anywhere. *Lamium maculatum,* the Spotted Dead Nettle, presenting purple flowers on 1-ft. stems in May, is the best member of the family and *L. m. aureum,* with golden leaves is attractive.

Propagation is by division in spring or autumn.

Lavandula (Lavender). Plantings of this dwarf aromatic shrub, with spikes of fragrant lavender-blue flowers in summer, often form a meeting place for slugs and snails. A light, well-drained soil containing lime and a sunny position suits this plant.

There are a number of varieties of the Old English Lavender *(Lavandula spica)* varying in height and depth of colour. The 1-ft. Hidcote, deep purple, is a good variety, and the dark lavender Munstead Dwarf, 15 in., is a great favourite. The blue, 3-ft. Grappenhall (if pruned after flowering and kept shapely) and *nana alba,* off-white, 6 in., have charm.

Propagation is by cuttings, under glass in August, or by heel cuttings rooted outside in October. It may also be increased by rooted shoots pulled off the base of an established plant.

Lavatera (Tree Mallow). The Tree Mallow bears pink panicles of saucer flowers in profusion and has downy leaves. It is sometimes slow to establish itself and dislikes disturbance.

Lavatera olbia rosea, given a special dry corner and kept shapely by spring pruning, will make a fine plant. The handsome pink flowers, borne on 5-ft. stems, appear from June to October.

Propagation is by seed sown in a cool greenhouse in spring and half-ripe cuttings rooted in a frame in mid-summer.

Lavender, see Lavandula
Lavender Cotton, see Santolina
Leadwort, see Ceratostigma
Leopard's Bane, see Doronicum
Liatris (Kansas Gay Feather, Button Snakeroot). This plant forms straight spikes of tightly packed reddish-purple flowers, opening from the top downwards. It is best planted in the spring in a moist soil and sunny position, the crown being positioned just below the surface.

Liatris pycnostachya has attractive rosy-purple spikes of some 3 ft., while *L. spicata* is a bluish-mauve dwarf of $1\frac{1}{2}$ ft. Both flower during summer and autumn.

Propagation is by division in the spring.

Lilium (Lily). This is a large and complex family of hardy and half-hardy bulbous plants about which it is difficult to generalise as to treatment as tastes vary. The majority require a well-drained soil to which decayed leafmould and sand have been added. The chances of the bulbs rotting is lessened if a sprinkling of silver sand is placed under each bulb when planting. They should be planted in October, set 6–8 in. deep in the case of stem-rooting kinds and 4–6 in. deep for others possessing only basal roots.

The lovely Madonna Lily, *L. candidum,* should be given rather special treatment. It should be planted in late July or early August in the open where it can get plenty of light and air, and it should be only lightly covered with soil to a depth of 1 in.

When buying bulbs from a specialist, the gardener should find out whether the lily in

Right: A summer border of phlox, *Salvia superba*, achillea, nepeta and other plants. Borders can be much enhanced by placing plants of different heights in juxtaposition to each other
Below: The herbaceous phlox Windsor, 3 ft., one of many attractive varieties of *Phlox paniculata*

question is tolerant of lime and its special demands.

Flower stems should not be cut down until the leaves turn yellow in the autumn, and a mulch of leafmould should be given in early spring. Every care must be taken to keep lilies healthy and bulbs suspected of disease should be burned at once.

I now mention a few of my favourites from a long list of beauties:

Lilium auratum, the Golden-rayed Lily of Japan, with immense gold-marked flowers in August and September; some of the hybrids are crimson-red, others almost vermilion, 4–8 ft.

L. bulbiferum croceum, orange with maroon spots. June and July flowering. Stem-rooting. 4 ft.

L. candidum, lovely white flowers in June, 5 ft.

L. henryi, deep orange-yellow, spotted brown. August flowering. Stem-rooting. 8 ft.

L. martagon, the Martagon or Turk's Cap Lily, with reflexed petals in shades of rose and light purple. June–July flowering, 4 ft.

L. regale, the Regal Lily, white, fragrant flowers, an easy doer and good town plant. July flowering. Stem-rooting. 6 ft.

Bottom left: The magnificent Golden-rayed Lily of Japan *Lilium auratum*, with beautifully marked flowers
Bottom right: the popular white-flowered Regal Lily, *Lilium regale*

L. speciosum, white, crimson-spotted flowers; slightly tender. August–September flowering. Stem-rooting. 4 ft.

L. testaceum, the well-known Nankeen Lily, apricot-yellow, with scarlet anthers and reflexed petals. July–August flowering. 4–6 ft.

L. tigrinum, the graceful Tiger Lily, orange-red with deep purple spots. July–September flowering. Stem-rooting. 4 ft.

Mid-Century Hybrids, a splendid June–July flowering group which includes such fine lilies as Enchantment, nasturtium red with small black spots, and Harmony, orange, chocolate spotted. Stem-rooting. 2–5 ft.

Propagation is by seed, by careful division of the bulb clusters in the autumn, or from individual plump scales broken from the bulb after flowering and placed in boxes of moist peat; or, in the case of certain species, such as *L. tigrinum,* by planting and growing the baby bulbs (bulbils) formed in the axils of leaves.

Lily, see Lilium
Lily-of-the-Valley, see Convallaria

Limonium (Statice, Sea Lavender). *Limonium latifolium* is an everlasting flower suitable for drying, with loose sprays of small, violet flowers. It should be given a well-drained soil and a sunny position.

The lavender-blue Blue Cloud, 2–3 ft., Violetta, violet-lilac, 2 ft., and Chilwell Beauty, violet, 2 ft., are among the best hybrids.

Propagation is by seed sown outdoors in March or April, but root cuttings of named varieties in autumn or winter are superior in performance.

Linaria (Toadflax). A large genus of which *Linaria purpurea,* 3 ft., and *L. pallida,* 2 in. and of a creeping habit, are the most frequently seen. These plants have small snapdragon-like, purple flowers in summer, *L. pallida* growing uninvited on walls and stony places in some parts of the country. *L. purpurea* Canon J. Went is a pink form that flowers over a long period.

Propagation is by division in spring or autumn. Seed may be sown outdoors in March or April.

Linum (Flax). This is a valuable garden genus, with flowers in white and yellow and many

delightful shades of blue. The linums are sun lovers, prepared to grow in the poorest of soils. *Linum arboreum,* yellow, a very small shrub of 15 in. with evergreen foliage and the more popular deep yellow *L. campanulatum,* 1 ft., are good garden plants. *L. narbonnense,* 1½ ft., is a pretty shade of blue, and *L. salsoloides nanum,* a pearl-white, prostrate grower. All are summer flowering.

Propagation is by seed sown outdoors in spring, or by division in spring.

Lithospermum (Gromwell). This is a low, spreading plant with flowers of glorious blue. It is a splendid rock garden plant of shrubby habit. *Lithospermum diffusum,* 1 ft., is a brilliant and intense blue. The deep blue *L. intermedium* (correctly called *Moltkia intermedia*), 9 in., is useful being more tolerant of lime than others of the genus. *Lithospermum purpureo-caeruleum,* with deep blue flowers in early summer, is a willing grower and, on occasion, rampant, but it lacks the star quality of *L. diffusum.*

Propagation is by cuttings of young shoots rooted in a frame in summer.

Lobelia. *Lobelia fulgens,* with striking scarlet flowers on 3-ft. stems in late summer, and purple foliage, is one of my favourite plants. It is hardy only in warm gardens and must be given protection through the winter in a cold frame. Given a rich leafmould compost it thrives in moist ground and even at the water's edge. There are some attractive varieties.

Lobelia fulgens Bees' Flame, with full spikes of scarlet flowers and purplish foliage; Kimbridge Beet, cerise with deep purple leaves, and *vedrariensis* with bright purple flowers and dark green foliage should be grown by those who have sheltered gardens in the South.

Propagation is by seed sown under glass in a temperature of 13°C. (55°F.) in March, or by division in spring.

London Pride, see Saxifraga

Loosestrife, see Lysimachia

Lupin, see Lupinus

Lupinus (Lupin). George Russell's hybrids sup-planted all previous forms of lupin, possessing a new brilliance and presenting a tremendous range of colour in June and July. Alas, they have not the stamina of the former species and plants require to be replaced every three or four years, but fortunately they flower as yearlings.

The lupins enjoy a sandy loam and have a dislike for lime, heavy clay, farmyard manure and over-rich soils. An open sunny position or a partially shaded border suits them well. They are best planted in the spring; old plants often resent disturbance.

The new Russell hybrid selfs and bicolors make their appearance every year, and Canary Bird, George Russell (an almost self-pink), Lilac Time, rosy lilac with white standards, flushed mauve, and violet-purple Thundercloud, one of the best of the dark purple varieties, are particularly worth growing.

The story that lupins revert to blue is unfounded, the truth being that the self-sown seedlings are aggressive and oust the more delicate and named varieties.

Mention must be made of *Lupinus arboreus,* the fragrant Tree Lupin, that forms a bush of some 4 to 5 ft. in height. Golden Spire, Mauve Queen and Snow Queen are all good varieties of this species easily raised from seed, or from basal cuttings taken in spring.

Propagation of Russell lupins is by division or by cuttings of 4–5 in. in length taken in March from the rootstock.

Lychnis (Campion). The lychnis are vivid perennials, some with the look of a wild flower. They do well in ordinary well-drained soil with a taste of manure.

Lychnis chalcedonica, 2–3 ft., the Maltese or Jerusalem Cross, is an old-fashioned plant with a bright scarlet, rounded flower head in summer, and rough oval leaves.

My favourite of this large family is *L. coronaria,* the Rose Campion, with furry, silver stems and foliage, and simple cerise flowers in July and August. *L. viscaria* (syn. *Viscaria viscosa*), 1½ ft., the German Catchfly, with grass-like foliage and

Pulsatilla vulgaris, the Pasque flower, a plant for a sunny, well-drained position

rosy flowers from May to July, also has its admirers.

Propagation is by seed sown outdoors in March or April or by division in spring or October.

Lysimachia (Loosestrife). Lysimachia is excellent for damp, shady places but it is an invasive plant that calls for control. The yellow or white flowers appear in summer.

Lysimachia clethroides, 3 ft., has graceful arching spikes of white blooms. *L. ephemerum,* 3 ft., will please those looking for grey foliage and grey-white flowers. *L. nummularia aurea,* 4 in., is the beloved Creeping Jenny, a plant within everybody's scope. *L. vulgaris,* 3 ft., the Yellow Loosestrife, with panicles of yellow flowers, is equally indestructible.

Propagation is by division in autumn or spring.

Lythrum (Purple Loosestrife). The lythrum has slender spikes of magenta flowers in July and August and is a plant that requires a moisture-retentive soil. *L. salicaria* Lady Sackville has flowers of a gay rosy-pink colour on $3\frac{1}{2}$-ft. stems. *L. virgatum* Robert, 2 ft., has grace and brilliant

rosy-red flowers, and *L. v.* Rose Queen bright pink blooms, $1\frac{1}{2}$–2 ft.

Propagation is by cuttings or division in spring.

Madwort, see Alyssum

Meadow Rue, see Thalictrum

Meconopsis (Tibetan Poppy, Himalayan Poppy, Welsh Poppy). There are a number of species of this attractive genus with light saucer-like flowers that nod in the wind. There are complaints that the meconopsis are short lived, but provided that they are given partial shade, a reasonably rich and moisture-retentive soil and are not allowed to dry out completely in summer or become water-logged in winter, they should survive for a number of years.

The outstanding species is surely *M. betonicifolia,* the Himalayan Blue Poppy, still known to many as *M. baileyi.* When first introduced it took the gardening world by storm. The flowers vary in colour from sky blue to a pinkish-lavender shade. It is not an easy plant to grow, is vulnerable to damp and must not be allowed to flower until mature and well established, otherwise it may give up the battle. Like all meconopsis it needs partial shade and prefers peat and leafmould to lime. Flowering in June and July, the plants grow from 3–5 ft.

Meconopsis cambrica, the yellow Welsh Poppy, with grey-green foliage, is an easy doer and a generous flowerer over a long period. Only 1–$1\frac{1}{2}$ ft., this poppy flowers continuously from May to August.

Poppy fans should give the purple poppy of Sikkim *(M. grandis),* the yellow Chinese Poppy *(M. integrifolia),* the red, purple or blue Satin Poppy *(M. napaulensis),* and the lavender Harebell Poppy *(M. quintuplinervia)* a trial. *M. integrifolia* and *M. napaulensis* are best treated as biennials (see p. 136).

Propagation is by seed carefully saved from the best-coloured plants.

Michaelmas Daisy, see Aster

Milfoil, see Achillea

Milkwood, see Euphorbia

Mimulus (Musk, Monkey Flower). This is a gay

Top left: Nevada, 7 ft. tall and perhaps the finest of all modern shrub roses, can be included in a mixed border
Bottom left: The tall floribunda rose Queen Elizabeth successfully used in a mixed planting

Top right: The gaiety and usefulness of the polyanthus has made them many friends. The stalwart Pacific Strain is shown here
Bottom right: *Liatris spicata* has purple cylindrical flower spikes which open from the top downwards

little plant with a look of the Snapdragon. It is a moisture lover and plenty of organic material should be added to the soil if it is to be long lived and happy. But now that the Musk has lost its scent it is fast losing popularity.

Mimulus cardinalis, the Crimson Monkey Flower, *M. c. grandiflorus* Rose Queen, 1 ft. bronzy scarlet, and Cerise Queen, 9 in., are showy plants for the front of the border, provided it is not too dry. They flower generously in June and July.

Mimulus cupreus has presented the gardener with an army of bright garden varieties of 8–12 in., flowering from June to September, including the small, bright tangerine hybrid Whitecroft Scarlet. *M. luteus,* 1 ft., the Monkey Musk, has yellow, red-spotted flowers.

Propagation is by seed or cuttings in spring or summer.

Monarda (Bee Balm, Bergamot). *Monarda didyma,* 2–3 ft., is another plant that depends on a moist soil. The nettle-like leaves are aromatic and the flower heads of red, mauve, pink and white are fragrant. The plant has a bushy habit and does well in sun or partial shade.

Bright scarlet *M. didyma* has been followed by a long list of desirable garden forms: Cambridge Scarlet, Croftway Pink, the scarlet Adam and the purple Prairie Night are helpful in giving colour from June to September.

Propagation is by division in spring or autumn.

Monkey Flower, see Mimulus

Montbretia. The attractive hybrids formerly known as montbretias are now named crocosmias (see p. 47).

Mullein, see Verbascum

Musk, see Mimulus

Nepeta (Catmint). This plant with mauve flowers and silver foliage is often used as a border edging. Provided the soil is well drained, it does well even on the poorest of soils and flowers almost the summer through. *Nepeta faassenii* is hardy but may die away during the winter on wet soil.

Nepeta fits in well with all softly coloured plants. Six Hills Giant, 2 ft., has erect flower spikes and is of a deeper and more violet shade.

Propagation is by division in March or by soft basal cuttings rooted in sandy soil in a frame. Plants cut down in July will send up suitable young growth from which cuttings can be made.

Obedient Plant, see Physostegia

Oenothera (Evening Primrose). The perennial species of oenothera flower over lengthy periods and the blooms stay open throughout the day. Happy in sun or shade and content with ordinary soil, provided it is not too parched, this is a useful plant for the front of the border.

Oenothera caespitosa, the tufted member of the family, is an almost prostrate grower. *O. fruticosa* is a bushy plant, providing a profusion of bright yellow flowers on stems up to 2 ft. from early summer onwards. Among the newcomers, Yellow River should not be missed, while the large, lemon *O. missouriensis* is a splendid dwarf species with yellow flowers in July.

Propagation is by seed sown in a cold frame in March or April, or cuttings taken in spring and rooted in sandy soil in a frame. Oenotheras which form tufts can be divided in early spring.

Paeonia (Peony). The herbaceous peony makes a rich contribution to the border and being as hardy as a polar bear once it has settled down is likely to outlive the gardener. Disliking disturbance they should be planted where they are to stay. The flowers are, in the main, white, pink, crimson and yellow.

A sunny or partially shaded place should be found for peonies and the soil very generously enriched with humus. Deep planting is to be avoided, and is often responsible for casualties or absence of bloom. When planting, the crown of the plant must not be allowed to be more than 2–3 in. below the soil's surface.

Gross feeders, peonies respond to a stable manure mulch in February and a dressing of bone-meal worked into the top 3 in. of soil in the autumn. They are remarkably free from disease, but should botrytis or wilt develop affected parts must be cut out and burnt and the plant sprayed with Bordeaux Mixture.

Top: *Monarda didyma* Croftway Pink,
the Bee Balm or Bergamot
Centre: *Oenothera missouriensis*, a dwarf
Evening Primrose and a belle of special quality for the
front of the border

Bottom: The delectable apple-blossom-coloured
Paeonia Sarah Bernhardt

There are a number of striking species. The June-flowering *P. emodi*, 2 ft., bears pure white flowers with golden stamens on graceful stems and is delightfully scented. *P. lactiflora*, 2 ft., with huge white single blooms of silky quality accompanied by handsome dark green foliage is the parent of a host of garden varieties known as the Chinese peonies. These are splendid garden plants in every way. The apple-blossom-coloured Sarah Bernhardt is one of the outstanding members of this group with beautiful double flowers; another is the flesh-pink Lady Alexandra Duff.

Paeonia officinalis, the red-flowered single peony, includes the cottage peonies in white, pink and sumptuous crimson.

The choice of varieties among the herbaceous peonies is bewildering and those interested in this genus should consult a peony specialist.

The Tree Peonies are shrubs that do well on chalk or other soils, provided they are well drained. *P. lutea ludlowii*, 6–8 ft., with beautiful yellow flowers has attractive divided, palm-like leaves of fresh green and this hybrid and also others of similar appearance would make a striking addition to any garden.

Propagation of the herbaceous peonies is by division in early spring. Species are increased by seed sown in sandy soil in boxes or pots in September and placed in a cold frame, and tree peonies by layering or grafting (not a practice for the amateur).

Papaver (Poppy). The two important garden poppies are the Oriental Poppy *(Papaver orientale)*, strong, handsome and growing to 3 ft., with generous foliage and immense flowers, nicely blotched in white, pink and scarlet, and the Iceland Poppy *(P. nudicaule)* with bright, fragile flower heads carried on 12–18-in. stalks. The flowers are yellow, orange to tangerine and white, plus the new, exciting pinks.

The Oriental Poppy is extremely hardy and I can recommend it to the unfortunate gardener who inherits a neglected, hungry border. In its barbaric fashion it has a special capacity for over-

Left: Seed heads, acanthus, euphorbia, allium and
lupin, from the autumn garden as well as hosta,
monstera and other foliage with the hybrid
tea rose Fragrant Cloud
in this lovely arrangement
by Sheila Macqueen

Below right: A form of *Trollius europaeus*, one of the
splendid Globe Flowers which provide
early summer colour

coming drought and starvation diet, often
becoming more difficult to oust than to grow. It
is interesting to note that the pimpernel and poppy
are the only two scarlet flowers native to this
country.

Poppies love the sun and provided the soil is
well drained they will give a good performance
on the poorest plot. It is best to stake the Oriental
Poppies because of their heavy heads and tendency
to sprawl.

The named varieties of *P. orientale* are legion,
growing $2\frac{1}{2}$–3 ft. Their flowering period, in May
and June, is apt to be short. Among the highlights are Barr's White; the blood-red Goliath;
deep brown-red Indian Chief; orange-scarlet Lord
Lambourne, with fringed edges; bright scarlet-
orange Marcus Perry, an immense flower; pink
Mrs. Perry; orange-red Stormtorch; and the
single cherry-rose Water Melon.

The Iceland Poppy is usually treated as a
biennial or annual due to its unhappy way of
dying out. The Kelmscott strain, flowering over a
long period in summer, is lovely and Tangerine
and Akarana Scarlet make grand cut flowers.

Propagation of Iceland Poppies is by seed sown
outdoors in May or June and of Oriental Poppies
by root cuttings of about 2 in. in length taken in
April or when lifting in the autumn and rooted in
a box of gritty compost.

Pasque Flower, see Pulsatilla

Pearl Everlasting, see Anaphalis

Penstemon (Beard Tongue). This plant is not
entirely hardy and is often short lived. Good
drainage and winter protection are essential in
cold parts of the country. There are dwarf and
shrubby species and a number of brightly-
coloured hybrids.

Penstemon barbatus bears tubular, foxglove-
shaped flowers of bright scarlet with pink throats
from June to August. Desirable hybrids that come
to mind are the clear pink Evelyn, 1 ft., and the
deep red Garnet, $1\frac{1}{2}$ ft.

Propagation is by seed sown in February to
provide plants for planting outdoors in May and
by cuttings made from basal shoots in September.

Peony, see Paeonia

Periwinkle, see Vinca

Peruvian Lily, see Alstroemeria

Phlox. The garden varieties derived from *Phlox
paniculata* play an important part in the border
from July to September. The huge fragrant
trusses come in white, pink, red, mauve and
magenta.

The phlox responds to good fare and plenty of
humus; it prefers a partially shaded position, and
moisture at the roots is essential to the plant. I
would suggest thoroughly soaking the soil during
a drought and mulching immediately afterwards
with spent hops.

Flower spikes, known as 'spokes', should be
restricted to four or six, and plants should be
divided after three years, the tired, woody core
being discarded.

Phlox are, unfortunately, vulnerable to eelworm, a pest invisible to the naked eye that
causes distortion of the stems and discoloration of
the foliage. The trouble is difficult to overcome
and it may be necessary to make a new bed.

Top: The low, mat-forming varieties of *Phlox subulata* are a delight in May and early June
Centre: The useful *Polygonum affine* which bears its spikes of pink flowers from August to October
Bottom: The scarlet, bladder-like calyces of *Physalis franchetii* make this a favourite

Captain Symons-Jeune has given us a host of splendid weather-resisting varieties, 1½–4 ft. in height, more lilac shaped and stylish than in the past, with evenly borne pips that overlap. Clear colours and sound constitutions have become the modern rule.

Orange-red Brigadier, salmon-pink Duchess of York (one of the best of the family), deep pink Lady C. Blose, and brilliant crimson Leo Schlageter are all outstanding.

It would be ungrateful not to put in a word for the rock garden phlox, the low, mat-forming *P. subulata* that covers itself with almost stemless blue, pink or white flowers in May or early June. Delightful and obliging it will crawl along the front of the border and can be easily increased after flowering by inserting cuttings in a sandy compost in a frame. The lilac-coloured variety G. F. Wilson has its cascades of narrow foliage completely hidden in the spring by mauve-blue star flowers each with immaculate blue spots at the base of the petals. G. F. Wilson is a good companion for Pink Delight or the rose Sensation.

Increase *P. paniculata* by cuttings taken from the base of the old plant in summer and rooted in a cold frame, or by division in October or March. Root cuttings, the best method of increase, should be taken early in the year as a precaution against eelworm. These should be rooted in a cold frame in February or March.

Phygelius (Cape Fuchsia). This is a semi-shrub with tubular and drooping scarlet flowers, requiring a warm position or the protection of a sunny wall. *Phygelius capensis coccinea,* the Cape Fuchsia, with bright red, yellow-throated flowers, blooms persistently through the summer.

Propagation is by half-ripe cuttings taken in mid-summer and rooted in a cold frame, or by seed sown under glass in March.

Physalis (Cape Gooseberry, Chinese Lantern). These are plants grown for their fruit and dried for winter decoration. Given a warm border the stems are fast to run underground and need controlling. *Physalis franchetii,* 2½ ft., with scarlet lanterns, is a favourite species.

Top: The Obedient Plant, *Physostegia virginiana* Vivid.
The rosy-crimson flowers appear in September
Bottom: Jacob's Ladder, *Polemonium coeruleum,*
an attractive plant with bright blue flowers, of which
there is also a white variety

Propagation is by division in the spring, or by seeds sown outdoors in April.

Physostegia (Obedient Plant). Most gardeners know the Obedient Plant, *Physostegia virginiana*. The common name comes from the strange characteristic of this plant. The flower remains put when pushed aside from the stem.

The Obedient Plant will grow in ordinary soil and prefers a partially shaded border.

Physostegia virginiana Vivid, rosy crimson, 2 ft., accompanied by Rose Bouquet, will give a welcome late September performance.

Propagation is by division in spring.

Pincushion Flower, see Scabiosa

Pink, see Dianthus

Plantain Lily, see Hosta

Platycodon (Chinese Bellflower, Balloon Flower). This plant has big, open, bell-shaped flowers in blue. It is an easy plant to please and is suitable for the front of the border.

Platycodon grandiflorus mariesii is smaller than the type (1 ft. tall as opposed to $1\frac{1}{2}$ ft.) with large flowers of deep blue in August and September. There is also a white variety, *albus,* and a semi-double variety, *plenus.*

Propagation is by seed sown under glass in a temperature of 13°C. (55°F.) in March or August or by division in spring.

Polemonium (Jacob's Ladder). This plant gets its common name from the ladder-like appearance of its pinnate leaves. It does well in ordinary soil but has no liking for excesses. There are a number of species of which *P. coeruleum* with panicles of blue or white flowers on stems of some 2 ft. is one of the most pleasing.

Propagation is by seed sown under glass in March or division in the autumn.

Polygonatum (Solomon's Seal). *Polygonatum multiflorum* is a graceful plant, 2–4 ft., with arching stems bearing tubular, creamy-white flowers in June, accompanied by very pleasant grey-green foliage. It is an excellent ground-cover plant for shady positions. There is an attractive double-flowered, variegated form and the perhaps less decorative, soft rose-pink *P. roseum.*

A study in soft colours. The plants include
aquilegias, onopordon, thalictrum, *Senecio laxifolius*,
olearia, *Papaver somniferum* and yellow-flowered verbascum

Propagation is by division of the roots in October or March.

Polygonum (Knotweed). This large, easy-going genus embraces several useful border plants that will succeed in almost any garden. *Polygonum affine,* with stiff 12-in. spikes of pink flowers and foliage that turns red-brown through the winter, has recently become fashionable. It is in flower between August and October. The variety Darjeeling Red is similar in many respects but the flowers are crimson. *P. amplexicaule speciosum* (syn. *P. a. atrosanguineum*) with lavender-like spikes of rich crimson on 4-ft. stems, robust and bushy, deserves to be seen more often but needs space.

Some species may be propagated by seed; all can be increased by division of roots in October or March.

Poppy, see Papaver

Poppy, Himalayan, Welsh, see Meconopsis

Potentilla (Cinquefoil). Content on poor soil, this plant is suitable for dry, sunny places. The flowers are white, yellow, orange and tangerine in colour.

Potentilla alba, 4 in., is pure white and mat forming and flowers from April to August. Gibson's Scarlet produces intense scarlet flowers on 12-in. stems from July to September; and the double, yellow blotched crimson Monsieur Rouillard, 18 in., are among the many good garden forms.

Propagation is by seed sown outdoors in spring or division in spring or autumn.

Primula. This lovely race of plants embraces the auricula, the charming Dusty Miller heavily powdered with meal, the cowslip, primrose and polyanthus.

I was an enthusiastic auricula fan and showman in my teens, growing the plants under glass to protect their farina, but the garden varieties such as Old Irish Blue have their own charm. Unfortunately, some of the named varieties are difficult to come by.

The blue primroses with immaculate yellow eyes have added glamour to their clan, while the Munstead strain of polyanthus and the tremendous stamina of the grand Giant Pacifics from California have increased the popularity of the family.

Among the many springtime beauties are *Primula denticulata,* the Drumstick Primula, with white, lilac and mauve orbs; *P. juliae* hybrids, in bright ruby and crimson shades, including the much admired claret-purple, dark-leaved Wanda, pink-flowered Garryarde Guinevere and the romantic Hose in Hose with leafy collars. But I remain faithful to my favourites, the double primroses, cream, parma violet and mauve: how I wish they were quicker to settle down and easier to please.

The primula family requires a moist soil and partial shade and enjoys an open, sandy loam with a high leafmould and peat content.

Propagation is by seed and division. *P. denticulata* is increased by root cuttings in early spring.

Pulsatilla (Pasque Flower). *Pulsatilla vulgaris,* formerly known as *Anemone pulsatilla,* is the enchanting mauve-violet Pasque Flower with golden stamens and filigree foliage. The fascinating buds are adorned with a silver surround of silky hair. This Easter, April-flowering plant is not particular about soil but enjoys a taste of chalk and needs a sunny, well-drained place.

P. v. rubra, white *Pulsatilla alpina* and light yellow *P. a. sulphurea* are full of charm, but alas not always long lived.

Propagation is by seed or division after flowering is over.

Purple Loosestrife, see Lythrum

Pyrethrum. This delightful daisy-like flower belonging to the chrysanthemum family comes in pink, red and white; some petals are tipped yellow. The singles are yellow centred. It is from the flower heads of this species that the insecticide pyrethrum is obtained.

Pyrethrums appreciate a light, well-drained soil and, from time to time, a mulch of well-rotted manure. If the soil is too rich the stems, becoming distorted, may lack the strength to support the weight of the large blooms.

Top: The poppy-like flowers of *Rommeya coulteri* with white petals and bold yellow stamens
Centre: Rosemary, *Rosmarinus officinalis*, the much-loved old-world evergreen shrub
Bottom: Black-eyed Susan, *Rudbeckia speciosa*, with orange-yellow, dark-centred flowers

This is a fortunate plant, its ferny foliage being less liable to attack from pests than the majority of insect-troubled chrysanthemums. The plants, particularly the singles, benefit by being cut back hard after flowering. They are around 2½–3 ft. in height.

The singles are more robust than the doubles and the hybridist has paid them more attention. From many attractive varieties of singles, my choice is Brenda, bright cerise; Bressingham Red, a large crimson; Eileen May Robinson, shell pink and excellent for cutting; Evenglow, salmon red; Kelway's Glorious, a vivid scarlet and one of the best; Marjorie Robinson, deep rose-pink; May Queen, pink and Silver Challenger, a fine white with a pink blush.

The doubles have centrally domed flowers surrounded by florets. Among the highlights are the pale pink Queen Mary; the rosy-carmine Vanessa; shell-pink Venus; and the pale pink Madeleine, as well as White Madeleine.

Propagation is by division in March. This late division may interfere with the season's flowering and the amateur gardener can afford to wait and lift in July, taking care that his plants do not dry out until established.

Ranunculus (Buttercup, Fair Maids of France). These are erect-growing plants with small, rosette, double flowers in white and the brightest of colours. They are indifferent to soil condition so long as it does not dry out completely in summer.

The white *Ranunculus aconitifolius* (Fair Maids of France) – superb in its double form – is completely hardy, but other species planted in cold gardens may be lifted in July and stored until late February or early March.

Propagation is by seed sown as soon as it is ripe in a cold frame, and by division in spring or October.

Red-hot Poker, see Kniphofia

Red Valerian, see Kentranthus

Rock Cress, see Arabis

Romneya (Californian Tree Poppy). This lovely plant, *Romneya coulteri,* has immense white, poppy-like flowers with telling golden stamens.

Growing to 6 ft., it flowers from July to September. This is a sun lover; it is content with poor stony soil provided it is well drained, but resents heavy, wet soil and disturbance, being slow to settle down. Once established it is fast to increase by underground runners, and it benefits by being cut down in late autumn or early spring.

Propagation is by seed sown in a greenhouse with a temperature of 13°C. (55°F.) in spring, or sections of root taken from established plants in spring.

Rosa (Rose). This is a varied family in form, shape, colour and habit due to the hybridisation carried out over centuries.

Hybrid tea blooms are nearly always double, the large, shapely flowers having many petals and usually being of splendid substance. The flowers, invariably borne singly, come in flushes with a resting period between bursts. The bushes grow to 2–4 ft.

Floribunda roses have smaller flowers that come in clusters and they flower continuously through-out the summer, making excellent bedding plants. Fast growing, from 2–4 ft., the floribunda is often a border-line hybrid tea but without quite the beauty or refinement of its forebears.

The dwarf polyanthas are bush roses of compact habit. The semi-single and double button flowers are borne in cluster-rambler formation on 15–18 in. bushes. Unfortunately, this group is vulnerable to mildew and carries little if any scent. The hybrid musks have a look of the floribunda but reach 7–8 ft. in height. Summer flowering, they give a fine autumn performance and their robustness makes them valuable.

The climbing roses, growing from 10–15 ft., have large flowers similar to those of the hybrid tea, do well against walls and have a fairly long flowering season. The ramblers, growing to 15 ft., are vigorous, have small flowers and are fashioned in clusters. They bloom but once, in June and July.

Miniature roses grow from 6–8 in. and are perfect replicas of their larger kinsmen.

The species and their hybrids, usually single flowered, are the wild roses and primogenitors of the moderns and there are over two hundred species to choose from. They are stylised and elegant and, with the nostalgic old roses, have a beauty beyond compare.

Roses are undemanding. They should be given a sunny position and do well on good loam or broken-up clay plus a bucket of manure. They are best planted in the second half of October or early November, but they can be moved at any time until the end of March when the weather is suitable. Some gardeners prune their plants in the autumn, but the general opinion holds that it is wiser to wait until the spring.

Propagation is by cuttings of firm young stems planted in autumn, or by budding in July.

Rose, see Rosa

Rosemary, see Rosmarinus

Rosmarinus (Rosemary). The common rose-mary, *Rosmarinus officinalis,* is an old-world ever-green shrub. It is hardy in most parts of the country but should be found a warm, well-drained corner.

There are a number of May-flowering, blue-mauve varieties in different shades, such as the 6-ft. *R. officinalis* Miss Jessop's Upright and the low-growing variety Severn Sea, and a white form, *albus.* Any pruning necessary should be done after flowering when the growth is young.

Propagation is by cuttings of half-ripened young shoots planted in a cold frame in August or September.

Rudbeckia (Cone Flower). These tall-growing, showy plants with yellow flowers have raised central discs in orange and black. They are happy in ordinary dryish soil if given a mulch of manure in the spring and plenty of sun.

The Hirta Hybrids, growing to 2 ft., are an excellent mixed strain giving welcome summer colour ranging from crimson and bronze to deep yellows. They are apt to be short lived and often best treated as annuals. *R. lacinata,* golden-yellow and autumn-flowering, is the tallest member of the genus at 5–8 ft. and a permanent resident. Its variety, the double-flowered Golden Glow, is also a long stayer reaching 6 ft. *R. sullivantii* Goldsturm, deep yellow, is another popular variety.

Rudbeckia speciosa (syn. *R. newmanii*), $2\frac{1}{2}$ ft., is the Black-eyed Susan, and has a bright orange-yellow flower with a dark centre that makes a useful bloom for cutting in summer.

Propagation is by seed sown outdoors in March or April, or by division of the roots in autumn or spring.

Sage, see Salvia

Salvia (Sage). The salvias are primarily herbs. They are a striking and interesting collection of plants that give a good display in a fine summer. There are over 500 species, some monocarpic, dying after flowering, while others are short lived. The gardener should be prepared with young plants to replace the departed.

Salvia sclarea, the Clary, has hairy stems and panicles of pale blue or pinkish flowers from June to September. I am particularly fond of *S. s. turkestanica,* with hooded blooms decorated by large rosy-lavender bracts, but my experience is that it is safer to treat the Clary as a biennial. One or possibly two plants growing to 3 ft. are helpful in giving character to a dull patch in the border.

Salvia superba is the most reliable of the hardy herbaceous group, with slender, purple flower spikes on $3\frac{1}{2}$-ft. stems in summer.

S. uliginosa, with spikes tipped with azure blue in late summer and early autumn, is worth trying in warm parts of the country where the soil is moist. It is a lovely true blue worth cosseting. 3–5 ft. It likes rich soil and a sunny border and should be cut down close to the ground in October.

Propagation is by division and plants should be divided every three years in spring or autumn.

Santolina (Lavender Cotton). These dwarf evergreen shrubs are suitable for a border edging in the same way as lavender. *Santolina chamae-cyparissus (S. incana)* has small, silver-felted leaves and yellow button summer flowers. Its foliage is especially handsome, as indeed is that of various other species, such as *S. neapolitana,* also silver

felted, and *S. virens,* with bright green foliage. All grow to $1\frac{1}{2}$–2 ft. These plants require a sunny position, good soil and annual pruning in spring.

Propagation is by summer cuttings of half-ripe shoots 2–3 in. long, with when possible, a heel attached, and inserted in sandy soil.

Saxifraga (Saxifrage, London Pride). *Saxifraga umbrosa,* London Pride, with green rosettes and spires of small flowers that create a foam of pink in spring, is welcome in any border. I would like to see more of the charming variegated and golden forms of the species.

Propagation is by division in spring or autumn.

Saxifrage, see Saxifraga

Scabiosa (Scabious, Pincushion Flower). The scabious is one of the most successful of the commercial cut flowers. It is not happy on a wet soil and has no liking for a heavy clay. It also resents disturbance and is better planted in the spring, never being allowed to dry out.

Scabiosa caucasica has flat, large, white or mauve flowers on slender 2–3-ft. stems, from June to September. The lavender-mauve Clive Greaves is a great favourite but there are a number of larger named varieties, in stronger or different colours. Among these are Moerheim Blue, violet-blue, and the blue Isaac House.

Propagation is by cuttings with a basal heel inserted in spring in sandy soil in a frame or greenhouse, or by seeds in spring under glass.

Scabious, see Scabiosa

Sea Holly, see Eryngium

Sea Lavender, see Limonium

Sea Pink, see Armeria

Sedum (Stonecrop). This large genus of succulent plants is, in the main, more suitable for rock gardens and walls than the herbaceous border. It will grow in almost any soil given a sunny position.

Sedum maximum atropurpureum is a useful late summer- and autumn-flowering variety for the front of the border, with thick spoon-shaped leaves of plum-red and pink flowers. It is a striking and altogether desirable subject, growing to 1–2 ft. in height.

Sedum spectabile, the bright pink species with glaucous foliage, is commonly grown and the floral 'platters' that appear in autumn have a fascination for Tortoiseshell and Red Admiral butterflies. The rose-salmon Autumn Joy, 2 ft., and the deep rose Brilliant, about 1½ ft., with wide heads of small flowers, make a splash of colour in September and October. William Robinson refers to these sedums in his book *The English Flower Garden* as the 'Everlasting Livelongs'.

Propagation is by division in spring or autumn.

Sempervivum (Houseleek). These plants have the gift of growing their rosettes on roofs and walls. They are sun lovers which can succeed with only a suspicion of soil. Sempervivums are easy plants to grow and especially suitable for the edge or rim of the border.

Sempervivum arachnoideum, the Cobweb Houseleek, has red flowers borne on 3-in. stems in July. *S. tectorum* is the common green houseleek that throws up a solid 3–3½-in. spike of purplish-red starry flowers, also in July.

Increase is by seed and cuttings of shoots or leaves inserted in a pan of fine soil at 16°C. (60°F.) in summer, or by offsets in spring. Also by division in spring.

Senecio. This is a tremendous genus that includes a number of plants we look upon as weeds. However, there are the silver-variegated perennial species that are welcome in the border, provided they are not allowed to trespass. Senecios are undemanding plants and are among the easiest to grow, enjoying a well-drained soil and sunshine.

There is a considerable amount of confusion about the shrubs *Senecio laxifolius* and *S. greyii* and it is the former which is readily obtainable and more usually seen. With its low-growing habit, attractive silver-grey foliage and yellow daisy flowers in summer, it is a useful evergreen shrub. *S. greyii* has soft green foliage and is inclined to be tender.

I must mention the shrubby *S. cineraria*, 1–2 ft., as it is an attractive silver plant. The pale yellow flowers are insignificant. It is also tender and likely to disappear in a hard winter. A tall herbaceous senecio is *S. tanguticus*, 5 ft., with yellow flowers in September–but it can spread disconcertingly. Another is the 4-ft. *S. przewalskii* (syn. *Ligularia przewalskii*) with yellow flowers in June and July and deeply divided leaves.

Propagation of the shrubby kinds is by half-ripe cuttings raised in a cold frame in late summer, the herbaceous kinds by division in spring or autumn.

Sneezeweed, see Helenium

Solidago (Golden Rod). This is rather a coarse-growing plant with long panicles of yellow flowers, easily pleased and with no special tastes. There are a number of species but the garden forms give a better account of themselves in the border.

Golden Gates, with bright yellow flowers paling at the tips, is one of the best varieties, flowering in July and August and growing to 2 ft. Golden Radiance has a long flowering period and Lemore, with flat heads of soft primrose in August and September, has an Award of Merit to its credit from The Royal Horticultural Society.

Propagation is easy by division in autumn or spring.

Solomon's Seal, see Polygonatum

Southernwood, see Artemisia

Speedwell, see Veronica

Spiderwort, see Tradescantia

Spire Lily, see Galtonia

Spurge, see Euphorbia

Stachys (Betony, Lamb's Ears). *Stachys lanata* is the star turn of this family, gardeners being devoted to the remarkably soft and silky-grey leaves. The red-purple flowers, borne in July, and the stems dressed in grey down have the same woolly texture. This is an indestructible, lovable plant of 1–1½ ft. that does well in the poorest of soils.

Another useful border plant is the Betony, *S. macrantha superba,* with handsome spikes of purple-violet flowers in May and June. This 1½-ft. plant with broad, hairy, deep green leaves spreads

Left: The Wood Lily, *Trillium grandiflorum*, a shade lover with snow-white flowers in spring
Right: The handsome flowers of the varieties of *Stokesia laevis* give pleasure in late summer and early autumn

quite rapidly and provides a good ground cover. Propagation is by division in spring.

Statice, see Limonium

Stokesia. This is a plant possessing handsome blue or mauve flowers not unlike those of a China Aster, but with an attractive white central base. The foliage is dark green and rather leathery.

Stokesias, which have a long flowering period in late summer and early autumn, are happy in sun or light shade and content with ordinary soil. There are several species such as mauve-purple *S. laevis,* but once again the garden forms are recommended including the varieties Blue Star, lavender-blue, and the deeper coloured Wyoming.

Propagation is by division of the roots in March or April.

Stonecrop, see Sedum

Sunflower, see Helianthus

Sun Rose, see Helianthemum

Thalictrum (Meadow Rue). This is an entrancing plant with leaves as fine cut as Maidenhair Fern and hosts of tiny, fairy-like flowers.

Unfussy about soil conditions, thalictrum will grow in sun or partial shade. Occasional mulches of well-rotted manure are rewarding but must be kept away from the crown of the plant.

There are a number of species and garden forms worth growing, among them *Thalictrum aquilegifolium*–the Columbine Meadow Rue –with greenish-yellow flowers borne on 4-ft. stems in June and July. *T. dipterocarpum*, 5 ft., is my pick of the family with graceful sprays of nodding lilac and yellow flowers from July to September. Its double form, Hewitt's Double, bears round, mauve flowers, and the white-flowered variety *album* is equally delightful. Slightly less tall, about 4 ft., is *T. rocquebrunianum,* with panicles of lavender-blue flowers in summer. *T. glaucum* has grey feathery foliage and pale yellow fluffy heads in summer. This subject grows from 4–5 ft.

Propagation is by seed or division in early spring.

Thrift, see Armeria

Thyme, see Thymus

Thymus (Thyme). This is a rock plant suitable for the rim of the border when old bricks are used instead of turf for edging. Thymes do well in light soil topdressed with sieved compost in the spring.

Many of the thymes hug the ground forming a dense, aromatic mat in different colours. Among these are the crimson *Thymus serpyllum coccineus*, *T. s.* Pink Chintz and the white *T. s. albus* that are a lovely sight in summer when they are in flower.

Thymus citriodorus aureus with golden leaves, and the lemon-scented *T. c.* Silver Queen are charmers of about 6–8 in. in height. *T. nitidus* makes an outstanding little grey-foliaged bush of 9 in. with soft pink flowers in June.

Propagation of the creeping kinds is by seed sown outdoors in April, by division in March or April, and of the shrubby types by cuttings rooted in a cold frame in July.

Tiarella (Foam Flower). This is a plant resembling the heucheras, and being almost a woodland subject is happy in a shady border where the soil does not dry out. *Heuchera brizoides* has, in fact, been crossed with *Tiarella cordifolia* to make *Heucherella tiarelloides*. It is known by some as the Foam Flower. *Tiarella cordifolia* with creamy-white flowers tinged with pink, has heart-shaped leaves spotted with red. Possessing a fast-running rootstock it makes an excellent carpeter. The May and June flowers are borne on 9-in. stems. *T. wherryi*, also about 9 in., has cream-apricot, beautifully scented flowers that may be enjoyed from May to September.

Propagation is by division of the roots in March or April.

Tick-seed, see Coreopsis

Toadflax, see Linaria

Torch Lily, see Kniphofia

Tradescantia (Spiderwort). This is a large genus but few of its members are entirely hardy. *Tradescantia virginiana* and its garden forms are dependable and easy to please, being indifferent to the soil conditions and happy in sun or shade. The flowers are three-petalled and of white, purple or pink colouring and the foliage grass-like. Osprey, 2 ft., a June to September flowering variety with large, white flowers that have fluffy blue centres, is outstanding.

Propagation is by division in spring.

Tree Mallow, see Lavatera

Trillium (Wood Lily). This is a lovely tuberous-rooted plant for a shady border, requiring a soil containing a good proportion of peat or leaf-mould. The single three-petalled flowers in white, pink or purple rise with dignity from the foliage.

Trillium erectum bears upturned, claret-coloured May flowers with pointed petals; *T. grandiflorum* is the familiar species with snow-white spring flowers, and *T. undulatum*, the Painted Wood Lily, has white spring flowers marked scarlet at the base of the petals and wavy, pointed leaves of copper brown.

Propagation is by careful division in March.

Trollius (Globe Flower). The round buttercup flowers in yellow or gold are a cheerful sight in early summer. The plants enjoy a well-cultivated, moist soil. On a visit to Denmark I saw a very successful tub-planting by the Copenhagen authorities of trollius and forget-me-nots.

Trollius europaeus is the parent of a number of bright varieties, among them the splendid 2-ft. Orange Globe.

Propagation is by division of the roots in autumn or spring, or by seed, which can be slow to germinate. Seed should be sown outdoors in shade in April or September.

Verbascum (Mullein). This is a tall, old-fashioned plant with gracefully tapering spikes of bloom, usually yellow or buff, but with an intriguing range of colours from biscuit to apricot and pink. The silver-grey foliage, in some cases soft and woolly, is an added attraction. Many of the verbascums are biennials (see p. 137), but there are some good perennials among them. They are easy to grow if given a light, well-drained soil and a sunny situation. Planting is best carried out in the spring.

Verbascum chaixii, 3 ft., the Nettled-leaved Mullein, is nicely felted and bears yellow flowers with striking purple filaments. *V. nigrum album*, 2–3 ft., has small white flowers with decorative purple centres, and *V. wiedemannianum* is outstanding with violet spikes on 4-ft. stems.

It is, however, the garden hybrids flowering from June onwards that distinguish themselves in the border. The soft primrose Gainsbrough, 4 ft., is one of the best of these. Pink Domino, White

Domino and Cotswold Gem, soft amber with a purple centre, have their admirers.

Propagation is by root cuttings 3–4 in. long taken in autumn or winter and lightly covered with sandy compost.

Veronica (Speedwell). This large, variable genus no longer includes the shrubby types, which are now known as Hebes. The herbaceous species, flowering from July to September, thrive in a good garden soil and a sunny position. Two of the most important are the robust *V. longifolia*, with slender spires of lilac-blue flowers on 3-ft. stems, and *V. spicata*, 1–1½ ft., which bears dense spikes of bright blue flowers and has narrow, oblong leaves.

There are any number of named garden forms derived from *V. spicata*, among them the rosy-red Barcarolle, 1½ ft., the pink Minuet and the taller pink Pavane.

Propagation is by division in autumn or spring or by cuttings in spring or early summer.

Vinca (Periwinkle). This trailing plant is excellent for furnishing a heavily shaded bare patch where nothing else will grow. It provides a mass of evergreen foliage and a few star-shaped flowers.

Vinca difformis bears pale lilac-blue flowers from November until Christmas, while *V. major* is a rampant grower which provides a fair number of blue flowers from May to September. *V. m. variegata* has green leaves blotched and margined with white.

Vinca minor, blooming from June to September, has smaller flowers and is more prostrate than *V. major*. There are white, purple, sky-blue and azure blue, double and variegated varieties in this group.

Propagation is by division in early spring.

Viola. This large family includes the pansy and violet. The viola is a compact plant and there are a number of species and named varieties in white, mauve, purple, apricot and yellow in a wide range of shades. This is a useful plant when a stop-gap is needed for the front of the border.

Violas do well in semi-shade and thrive in a rather moist loam. Dead-heading is a 'must' if the plants are to go on flowering throughout the summer.

Viola cornuta, the blue Horned Violet from the Pyrenees, is the parent of many of the garden violas or tufted pansies, and the long-flowering miniature violettas, among them the gay orange-yellow Buttercup, the violet-blue Hansa, and the violet-purple Lady Sackville.

Viola gracilis, with leafy stems and large violet flowers, is a continuous flowerer and one of the highlights of the group. Its hybrids and varieties such as *alba*, Black Knight, *lutea* and the rich-violet *major* are well worth growing.

The named garden forms such as Arkwright's Ruby, the apricot Chantryland, that has a dash of pink; the pale yellow Dawn, and the magenta Miss Brookes are also desirable.

Propagation is by seed sown in boxes in spring and placed in a shaded frame, or by cuttings (to increase named varieties). The plants should be cut down to ground level in August and top-dressed with leafmould. They will then produce strong growth from which cuttings can be made. Shoots which have not flowered should be selected and these can be rooted in a frame.

Pansies, more straggling in habit than the violas, are usually treated as annuals and raised from seed. The flower bears a dark central blotch which distinguishes it from the viola.

Viola odorata is the sweet-scented violet which thrives on leafmould and decomposed manure. It should not be allowed to flower before it is well established. Princess of Wales, with immense violet-coloured flowers, is excellent for picking but it is, unfortunately, far less grown now that buttonholes are no longer fashionable.

Propagation is by runners taken from the parent plant in early autumn.

Virgin's Bower, see Clematis

Wallflower, see Cheiranthus

Welsh Poppy, see Meconopsis

Windflower, see Anemone

Wood Lily, see Trillium

Wormwood, see Artemisia

Yarrow, see Achillea

Part Two

Annuals

Introduction to Hardy Annuals

The gardener intent on keeping his border gay from June to October must inevitably plant a mixed border of annuals and perennials. This should not prevent him from planting a special border of annuals only, or extra beds for the flower arranger where she can enjoy the liberty of cutting fancy free.

An annual is a plant that completes its life cycle within the space of a year. Some of the plants we know as annuals may well be biennial or perennial in their native land due to a different or warmer climate.

The true annuals have a short life and a brief growing season. They are always in a hurry to mature, set seed and fulfil themselves, and in some cases manage to complete the cycle within the space of a few weeks. The flowers are bright and dazzling in colour, the purpose being to attract the attention of insects near and far, so securing quick fertilisation and seed setting.

Annuals are, in the main, summer plants germinating in the spring and departing in September or October with the arrival of the frosts. But there are those best sown in the autumn to over-winter in the border as seedlings, where they give an earlier and finer performance.

Some annuals are hardier than others, and those which are autumn sown require to be tough plants capable of standing up to sharp frost. Among these are the cornflower, larkspur, marigold and nigella. In fairness to the novice I should add there is always a certain risk about autumn sowing, success depending, as it does, on reasonable weather.

Anyone wishing to see annuals at their best should visit The Royal Horticultural Society's Garden at Wisley, Surrey. The annual border there, of impressive dimensions, is unsurpassed in brilliance of colour and variety throughout the summer months.

Cultivation of Hardy Annuals

The majority of annuals love the sun. They should be given an open position and well-drained soil. A broken-down loam or an ordinary fairly rich garden soil will suit them well.

Over-light and poor soil should be enriched with well-rotted manure in the autumn, and heavy soil lightened by deep digging, adding leaf-mould, peat and crushed mortar rubble and lime if called for. If farmyard manure cannot be obtained, a light dressing of general fertiliser should be forked into the surface of the soil during the spring. But it should be stressed that over-rich soil is a mistake leading to exuberant foliage and few flowers.

If the soil has been well dug in the autumn the wind, rain and frost will have done much to break down the clods, and all that will be needed is a hoe and rake to get a fine tilth.

When to Sow

March is a good sowing month for those living in the South, but northern gardeners would be wise to wait until April. There is, however, a danger in delaying too long for as the sun gains power so the soil dries out faster, and young seedlings are vulnerable to drying spring winds and drought.

Small seeds can be sown broadcast and lightly raked in while drills should be drawn for the larger seeds. The command on the packet to sow thinly is easier said than obeyed, but if achieved it will save the gardener the tiresome job of thinning out later on. A still day should be chosen for sowing, it being quite impossible to distribute the seed satisfactorily in a wind.

Small seeds should be sprinkled over with only a suspicion of finely sieved soil: large seeds such as those of nasturtiums or sweet peas should be covered with about 1½ in. of soil. A brushwood barrage placed over the seed bed gives some protection against birds, cats and dogs, but it must be removed immediately the seedlings make

their appearance, otherwise they will grow weak and leggy in their efforts to reach the light.

Thinning and Transplanting

The first thinning should be done when the seedlings are large enough to handle comfortably, and second and third thinnings will ensure that they have room to reach their natural spread.

A large number of seedlings will transplant if the move is made at an early stage and on a dullish showery day. But some, such as poppies and eschscholzias, are not transplantable.

The gardener can usefully collect and sow seed from species, but seed from varieties and hybrids cannot be relied upon to come true to type. Seed pods should be gathered when ripe and dry, laid on a tray and stored in an airy, dry place to finish their ripening. Finally, the seed should be placed in an air-tight tin until sowing time.

Attractive Hardy Annuals

Acroclinium. This is a long-stemmed everlasting flower with attractive semi-double flowers in rose, pink and white. The mixtures usually offered derive from *Acroclinium roseum,* which is more correctly known as *Helipterum roseum* but is usually listed under its former name. Height, 15–18 in. Seed may be sown in the border in April where the plants are to flower.

Agrostemma (Rose of Heaven). *Agrostemma* Milas is an improved variety with large, soft lilac-pink flowers possessing white centres as much as 2–2½ in. across. The flowers are borne on wiry 3- to 4-ft. stems from June to September and are useful for cutting, remaining open come sun or rain.

Seeds should be sown in March and April, and the seedlings transplanted later if necessary.

Alyssum (Sweet Alyssum). The botanists have reallocated the Sweet Alyssums (varieties of *Alyssum maritimum*) to the genus *Lobularia,* but gardeners are unwilling to accept their old favourite under its new name. This is a popular edging plant with a love of the seaside and, although perennial, is best treated as an annual.

Snow Carpet, 3–4 in., Little Dorrit, 6 in., and *minimum,* suitable for crevice or paving, 2–3 in. are a desirable white trio. Rosie O'Day, lilac-pink, 4 in.; Royal Carpet, purple, 3–4 in., and Violet Queen, 4–6 in. are also good varieties.

Seeds should be sown in April or in autumn if early flowers be desired. Seedlings can be transplanted if necessary.

Amaranthus (Love-Lies-Bleeding, Prince's Feather). The amaranthus is a fascinating old English border plant, introduced to this country from the Tropics at the end of the sixteenth century, that has recently come back into fashion. Adorned with drooping velvet tassels of deep crimson (or green), this is a plant of outstanding ornamental value. Love-Lies-Bleeding *(Amaranthus caudatus)* and Prince's Feather *(A. hypochondriacus)* are hardy annuals but all the other members of the genus are half-hardy (some of these are referred to on p. 113).

Amaranthus caudatus has effective dark red racemes but I have a weakness for *A. c. viridis* with green tassels that should delight the flower arranger. These two are some 3 ft. in height. *A. hypochondriacus* is about half this height.

Seed should be sown outdoors in April or May where the plants are to flower.

Anchusa. *Anchusa capensis* is a biennial best grown as a hardy annual. Blue Bird, an indigo-blue variety, 15 in., has a look of the Forget-me-Not.

The seeds should be sown in March or April, but in cold areas the gardener should wait until severe winter weather is over before sowing.

Apple of Peru, see Nicandra

Asperula (Woodruff). *Asperula azurea setosa* (botanically now known as *A. orientalis* but still listed in catalogues under its former name) is sky blue and bristly. The small linear leaves are studded with clusters of tiny four-petalled flowers on 9-in. stems said to have the scent of new-mown hay–but, as always with scent, this is a matter of opinion. Seeds should be sown in April.

Baby Blue Eyes, see Nemophila

Baby's Breath, see Gypsophila

Blazing Star, see Mentzelia

Cabbage and Kale, Ornamental. Ornamental cabbage and kale are now greatly favoured by the flower arranger, being of a unique texture whether curled, fringed or multi-coloured.

Seeds of ornamental summer varieties sown in a cold frame during January will provide early crops. Or seed may be sown in April or May in prepared beds, moving young plants to their flowering positions in June. If the seed bed is dry it should be soaked the night before transplanting and the roots dipped in a puddle of soil and water before planting. Cabbage does well on ground that has been manured for a previous crop. Firm planting should be the rule. Grown in this way the plants will mature by late summer.

Calendula (Garden or Pot Marigold). Varieties of *Calendula officinalis* are foolproof continuous-flowering annuals, sun lovers prepared to grow in almost any soil. Mr. David Burpee, the well-known Californian seedsman, has sought to make the Marigold America's national flower, offering a generous reward for a pure white variety. Meanwhile, there are many shades of orange, apricot, yellow and cream flowers in single and double forms, $1\frac{1}{2}$–2 ft., with quilled or tubular petals and, on occasion, different coloured centres.

Seeds can be sown in spring or September, preferably the latter to obtain flowers in early summer.

Californian Poppy, see Eschscholzia

Candytuft, see Iberis

Catchfly, see Silene

Centaurea (Cornflower, Sweet Sultan). The bright blue *Centaurea cyanus*, growing to 3–4 ft., has red, pink, lilac, deep and pale blue and white varieties, as well as polka-dotted and dwarf kinds of only 1 ft. Unfortunately, the doubles seem to have mislaid some of the family charm.

Centaurea moschata, the purple-lilac Sweet Sultan, with thistle-like heads, fringed and slightly scented, and the yellow *C. m. flava,* are fine border annuals. The *imperialis* strain, including deep violet, purple, pink and white, fragrant varieties have an old-fashioned air about them. The large blooms on 2-ft. stems are excellent for cutting.

Seeds may be sown in March or April for June to September flowering and from August to October for May flowering.

Chinese Houses, see Collinsia

Chrysanthemum. The splendid hardy, annual species of *Chrysanthemum* are perhaps a little underrated. Thriving in good garden soils and sunny situations, they flower freely all summer. Varieties of *Chrysanthemum carinatum* (syn. *C. tricolor*) are very showy with single, white, daisy-like flowers 2 in. across that have bright coloured rings at the base of the petals and purple centres. Monarch Court Jesters, $1\frac{1}{2}$ ft., is a lively strain of dwarf chrysanthemum that has come to stay.

These flower from June to September, have an attractive range of colours and are good for cutting. *C. coronarium* is represented by yellow and white doubles and semi-doubles and the single canary-yellow Golden Glory with a central disc to match.

I must put in a word for *C. inodorum*, more correctly known as *Matricaria inodora,* usually found in the seed catalogues under the heading chrysanthemum. Bridal Robe is a variety of this species with snow-white, double flowers on 9-in. stems. Another annual chrysanthemum worth trying is the newcomer *C. segetum* Paradiso, bravely indifferent to the weather and presenting a profusion of lemon flowers with black central discs.

These annual chrysanthemums should be sown in April where the plants are to flower, gradually thinning out the resulting seedlings to 1 ft. apart.

Clarkia. This is an extremely hardy plant and a great favourite, with slender spikes of double flowers in pink, red or white. Unfussy about soil, clarkias grow well in sunny or partially shaded places.

Clarkia elegans is the parent of a number of purple, orange-scarlet, crimson, salmon-pink and white double varieties, flowering from July to September. Most grow to 2 ft. tall, some a little less. *C. pulchella,* with lilac to white flowers on $1\frac{1}{2}$-ft. stems, is less stalwart than *elegans,* but fits in with almost any colour scheme. There is a dwarf variety, Tom Thumb, 1 ft., in purple and other colours.

Seeds should be sown in March or April where the plants are to flower.

Collinsia (Chinese Houses). This is a plant with small bell-shaped flowers in white, blue and pink, suitable for the front of the border or as an edging. It thrives on all soils in sun or partial shade.

Collinsia bicolor (syn. *C. heterophylla*), 15 in., has clusters of white flowers with rose, lilac or purple markings. *C. grandiflora,* 12 in., possesses a becoming deep blue lower lip, the top lip varying from white to purple.

Top: Chrysanthemum segetum, a showy and profusely
flowering annual chrysanthemum
Bottom: Convolvulus tricolor with funnel-shaped
flowers of deep blue, white and yellow

Overleaf: A riot of colour from eschscholzias,
the Californian Poppies. These popular flowers are
among the gayest of all annuals

Seeds can be sown from March to May, or in
September if an early display of blooms is desired.
Convolvulus. This is a plant with a semi-trailing,
sprawling habit, useful for growing in baskets.
One plant can have a spread of 1½–2 ft. There
are fine blues, pinks and crimsons.

A dry, ordinary or even poor soil will satisfy
the convolvulus provided it is given a warm,
sunny position.

Convolvulus tricolor (C. minor), 12 in., has
bright deep blue, funnel-shaped trumpet flowers
with a white base and a central yellow eye. Drifts
of the variety Cambridge Blue and ultramarine-
blue Royal Ensign make a vivid planting. There
are also pink and crimson varieties, some with
contrasting silver foliage.

Sowings can be made in March, April or
September.

Cornflower, see Centaurea

Delphinium (Larkspur). Many of the modern
Larkspurs have been developed from *Delphinium
ajacis,* the Rocket Larkspur, and have inherited its
way of growth, the single stem with secondary
branches. The erect spikes of closely formed
flowers are in pink, lilac, rosy scarlet, mauve and
white and provide colour in the border from June
to September.

Larkspurs enjoy rich, moist soil and plenty of
sunshine.

The Giant Imperial varieties with double
flowers, 3–4 ft., evolved from *D. consolida,*
are splendid border plants, good for cutting. The
Regal and Supreme types now being introduced
from America are an improvement on the Giants
being slightly taller and bearing superior spikes.
The dwarfs, varieties of *D. grandiflorum*, 1–1½ ft.,
are usually grown as half-hardy annuals and
flower from July to September; unlike their big
brothers the dwarfs transplant well.

In the case of all but the last-mentioned, seeds
may be sown in autumn or spring where the
plants are to flower. Larkspurs seldom transplant
satisfactorily. The seed germinates slowly and
uncertainly in hot, dry soil.

Dracocephalum (Dragon's Head). This willing

Top: The handsome Quaking Grass, *Briza maxima*, with nodding spikelets of green and white
Bottom: *Godetia* Sybil Sherwood, a salmon-pink, white-edged dwarf variety

plant, flowering from July to September, deserves to be seen more. The flowers are open mouthed and sweet scented. A light, ordinary soil and a partially shady border will suit the Dragon's Head.

Dracocephalum moldavica, with leafy spires of purple, violet or white flowers and lemon-scented foliage, the outstanding species of the family, is quite irresistible to the bee.

Seeds should be sown in spring.

Dragon's Head, see Dracocephalum

Echium (Viper's Bugloss). This valuable annual, flowering from June to September, is content with dry and poor soils, but must be found a sunny position.

Echium creticum with soft red flowers on $1\frac{1}{2}$-ft. stems and *E. plantagineum*, pink, red and blue, are both rewarding. The variety Blue Bedder has made its name as a reliable free flowerer. Meanwhile, the dwarf hybrids, 15–18 in., should not be missed.

Emilia (The Tassel Flower). *Emilia flammea* (syn. *E. saggitata*), flowering from June to September or October, bears clusters of small orange-red tassels on long stems. The variety *aurea* has golden-yellow flowers. This is another easy-going plant for a dry position. Height $1\frac{1}{2}$–2 ft.

Seeds should be sown in March or April.

Eschscholzia (Californian Poppy). One of the gayest of the annuals and very easily grown, the eschscholzias make no special demands. Although they are inclined to sprawl they can be kept reasonably tidy.

Eschscholzia caespitosa, tufted and with bright yellow flowers, is ideal for the odd gap in the front of the border. It is only 6 in. tall. *E. californica* has grey, feathery foliage and is a species which has provided a mixed bag of splendid varieties. The single eschscholzia is to be had in a number of brilliant colours separately packeted. The doubles and semi-doubles are vivid, frilled and fluted. All have the magical gift of flinging themselves wide open at the sight of the sun. Named varieties include Carmine King, Orange King, yellow Chrome Queen and Dazzler, scarlet, all about 1 ft. The Monarch Art Shades mixture, flowering from June to September, has become extremely popular.

March or April sowings should be made where the plants are to flower. Seedlings should be carefully thinned to 8 in. apart.

Flax, see Linum

Gilia. This is a pincushion-like flower with finely cut foliage, flowering from June to September. The gilia should be given an open position and an ordinary light garden soil.

Gilia achilleifolia has pale lavender, funnel-shaped flowers on 1-ft. stems; there are also white and rose forms. *G. androsacea*, 2–2½ ft., has star-like flowers in rose, lilac and white. *G. capitata*, one of the best known species, has long stems bearing light blue flower heads, and fern-like foliage, while *G. dianthoides* (syn. *Fenzlia dianthoides*), is a perfect dwarf and its lilac or pale rose flowers, borne in clusters, are spotted with violet. *G. liniflora* is more impressive than the dwarfs with large white or blush flowers on 12- to 15-in. stems, and *G. lutea*, the Leptosiphon, is smothered in star-like flowers on 6- to 9-in. stems. *G. tricolor*, 1–1¼ ft., commonly known as Bird's Eyes, has lavender and white flowers brightened by gold and purple centres. The flowering period is between June and September.

Seeds of the taller and tougher members of the genus should be sown in September to over-winter; the dwarfs are best spring sown.

Godetia. The large flowers of the godetias vary in colour from white to rose-red. The lovely free-flowering modern hybrids have almost ousted the species that are now rarely seen.

Godetias are happy in any ordinary soil, in sun or partial shade. The tall, double hybrids—about 3 ft.—have a tendency to snap off at ground level and for safety should be supported by light brushwood twigs. Rosy Morn, deep pink, is a delightful example of this type, 3 ft.

The dwarf varieties, 9–18 in., have large single and double flowers. The cherry-crimson Vivid is a striking variety, white at the base of its petals. Sybil Sherwood, salmon-pink, white

edged, and Lavender Queen are among my favourites.

Seed should be sown in March, April or September. The seedlings must be severely thinned to avoid legginess. They do not take kindly to transplanting.

Grasses (ornamental species). Grasses are becoming increasingly popular with the flower arranger. Once these grasses have been carefully dried they can be used in winter bouquets together with ever-lasting flowers. The spikes should be cut before the seed has ripened and hung up to dry.

The hardy group include *Agrostis nebulosa*, the Cloud Grass, with delicate branching heads on 1½-ft. stems; *Briza maxima*, the Quaking Grass, and quite my favourite genus with nodding spike-lets of green and white; *Hordeum jubatum*, the Squirrel-Tail Grass, silky and long haired, which has barley-like tassels: *Lagurus ovatus*, the Hare's Tail Grass, with soft-plumed and woolly heads carried on long 1½-ft. stems; and *Setaria italica*, a Foxtail Millet type of grass which gracefully nods large yellow-green flower heads on 1½ to 2-ft. stems.

Sow between March and May.

Gypsophila (Baby's Breath). The annual gypsophila, 1½ ft., is derived from *Gypsophila elegans*, and is a free-branching sprawler with larger flowers than those of the perennial group. The flowers are borne throughout the summer, and to be effective, plants should be sown in bold drifts.

This gypsophila is a chalk lover, content on most well-drained soils but quick to succumb if conditions are excessively wet.

Gypsophila elegans alba is a useful white cut flower. Covent Garden has extra large white flowers and *G. e. rosea* is the pink form.

Seeds of these plants should be sown from March to July.

Iberis (Candytuft). Iberis is one of the easiest and most useful quick-growing annuals with flowers in white, pink and all shades of mauve, purple and crimson. It does well in a sunny position in ordinary garden soil.

Right: Centaurea Polka Dot, a dwarf, bushy cornflower
with especial charm
Below: Limnanthes douglasii, the Meadow Foam, is
a useful early-flowering annual

Iberis amara coronaria, the Rocket or Hyacinth-flowered Candytuft, is of erect habit, 15 in. tall, and the long spikes of white flowers are slightly fragrant. *I. umbellata,* the Globe or Common Candytuft, 6–15 in. tall, bears clusters of rose, mauve, purple or white heads. There is also a group of dwarf hybrids, 6–9 in.

Sowings can be made in autumn or spring, to have flowers from early summer to September.

Larkspur, see Delphinium

Lathyrus (Sweet Pea). The modern sweet pea, derived from *Lathyrus odoratus,* is too well known to need description. It has an ever-extending colour range.

If a cold frame is available, the plants are best raised by autumn sowing, and gardeners on heavy, wet soil are advised to sow about the end of November. The seed may be sown in pots or boxes, and as soon as germinated should be given plenty of ventilation while being protected from frost. The seedlings can be planted out in April after being carefully hardened off. Firm planting is important.

The soil should be deeply dug some months before planting; a mixture of four parts clean top soil, one part leafmould or peat, and one part sand is ideal for sweet peas. Over-manuring is to be avoided. The alternative, for those living in warm areas but without a frame, is outdoor sowing in March. Gardeners in colder districts should wait until April before sowing.

If large blooms are wanted, the plants should be grown on the cordon system, restricting each plant to a single stem and regularly pinching out all side growths and tendrils while tying the leader to a tall cane. When the single stem, half way through the season, has reached the top of the cane, its life can be prolonged by layering. This entails untying the plant, laying it along the ground past three or four canes and then curving the stem up gently to the next cane. The plant will now reach up to perhaps 2 ft. and, gaining a new lease of life, will flower on for some weeks.

The second method, that results in small flowers, is bush planting, allowing the plants to go much their own way supported by a few twiggy branches.

Sweet peas are vulnerable to greenfly and should be sprayed immediately the pest is spotted. Too much moisture at the roots of young plants is dangerous, yet once established care must be taken that they do not dry out.

Bud dropping, often due to hot days followed by cold nights, is disappointing but not a disease, and the trouble will right itself as the weather becomes more settled.

There are a number of splendid varieties that stay in my mind such as carmine Carlotta, cherry-red and white Percy Izzard, lilac Leamington, mauve Elizabeth Taylor, almond-pink Viscount, salmon-pink and white Superfine, cerise-scarlet Air Warden, White Ensign and Swan Lake, both pure white, and the lavender Gertrude Tingay.

The Galaxy strain with up to seven flowers to a stem are splendid for cutting. The plants are strong and vigorous but are not recommended for growing as cordons. Also popular nowadays are the early-flowering dwarf Bijou strain, only 15–

18 in. with large, frilled flowers borne freely, making them splendid edging plants. The Little Sweetheart strain consisting of bushy little plants of only 8 in. is especially suitable for window-boxes.

Lavatera (Mallow). This is one of the best annuals we possess with maple-like leaves and large, trumpet-shaped pink and white flowers that form in the axils of the leaves and at the end of the sprays from July to September. Lavateras should be given a sunny place and, if possible, a fresh position every year to prevent the building up of disease. They are plants which grow well in a light rich soil.

Lavatera trimestris, 3 ft., is a handsome plant with pink flowers some 4 in. in diameter; there is also a white form, *alba*. The variety known as *splendens* has larger white flowers and a tidier habit; Loveliness, 2 ft., has rose-pink flowers while Sunset, of similar height, has deep rose flowers. Aurora, a bright, striped rose-pink variety with even larger flowers than Loveliness is offered by some seedsmen.

Seeds should be sown in spring where the plants are to flower for the seedlings seldom transplant well.

Layia (Tidy-tips). Layia is another yellow daisy flower, but on this occasion neatly tipped white. A sun lover of easy culture from western North America, it is happy in ordinary soil. *Layia elegans*, tipped white or cream, is the member of the genus most often seen, and there is a pleasing, completely white petalled form named *alba*. The flowering period is from July to September.

Seeds are sown in March or April where the plants are to flower.

Limnanthes (Meadow Foam). The dwarf, yellow and white 'scrambled egg' plant *Limnanthes douglasii*, or Meadow Foam, 6 in., is a useful early flowerer. Although a native of California it is a real tough. It will grow almost anywhere for anybody, sowing itself with great generosity in moist, light soils. It gives an abundance of small, white-centred yellow flowers. It can be had in flower from June to October.

Sowings can be made in spring or autumn.

Linaria (Toadflax). The small snapdragon-like flowers of linaria are to be had in a large variety of colours, from blue to red, pink, yellow and white. Toadflaxes are easily grown but surpass themselves in a sunny position and a light well-drained soil. However, they can be relied upon to make the best of whatever is given them.

Linarias are quick to seed and the faded flowers must be cut back if a prolonged flowering period from June to September is desired.

Linaria maroccana, 9 in., is a violet-purple Moroccan species from which improved strains

Far left: The Scarlet Flax, *Linum grandiflorum rubrum*
Left: Baby Blue Eyes, *Nemophila insignis,* which can be had in flower throughout the summer

have been derived. The Excelsior hybrids are, in effect, long-spurred miniature snapdragons in bright shades, and the Fairy Bouquet strain is even more compact, only 9 in., and includes a splendid range of colours.

Seeds should be sown in March or April where the plants are to flower. The seeds are tiny and should be sown as thinly as possible.

Linum (Flax). Flax is easy to please and succeeds on poor soil if given a sunny situation. An especially fine variety is *Linum grandiflorum rubrum,* the Scarlet Flax, with brilliant scarlet flowers on 12-in. stems. The white form, Bright Eyes, is centrally marked with crimson. *L. usitatissimum,* the Common Flax, is tall, slender and delightful, with blue flowers on 1½- to 2-ft. stems.

Sowings can be made from March to May to provide a succession of flowers throughout the summer to September.

Love-in-a-Mist, see Nigella
Love-Lies-Bleeding, see Amaranthus
Lupin, see Lupinus
Lupinus (Lupin). I am surprised that the annual lupin is not grown more often. It is smaller than the perennial kinds and the spikes are shorter, but it is certainly a poor relation worth cultivating. Annual lupins are easily grown in a sunny or partially shaded border in ordinary soil, but they have no liking for chalk.

There are innumerable species of which *Lupinus hartwegii* is the most outstanding, bearing blue and white flower spikes, and distinctive soft hairy foliage. The garden strains, 2½ ft., and white, sky and dark blue and rose in colour, should be seen more often. The flowers appear from July to September.

Pixie Delight, the dwarf strain, comes in a variety of colours and shades.

Sowings should be made in April or May where the plants are to flower.

Malcomia (Virginian Stock). Virginian stocks–mixtures derived from *Malcomia maritima*–make perfect edging plants. They include such colours as red, pink, lilac and white, and the confetti-like flowers are borne profusely and continuously

throughout the summer. Although seed is usually sown in mixture, named varieties like Crimson King, 9 in., and the smaller red and white Tom Thumb, 6 in., are available separately.

Sowings can be made in spring or September.

Mallow, see Lavatera

Malope. Malope is a bushy plant resembling the lavatera (see p.106). The flowers are funnel-shaped and as they are of a rather hard magenta colour the plants should be carefully placed to avoid any clashing with neighbours. This is an easy plant to grow, satisfied with ordinary garden soil if given a sunny situation.

The rosy-purple *Malope trifida* is a showy species with white and pink forms. Aphrodite, carmine-red, is a colourful variety and mixtures are available from many seedsmen. All reach 2–3 ft. and flower from July to September.

Sowing should be done in April and May.

Marigold, Garden or Pot, see Calendula

Meadow Foam, see Limnanthes

Mentzelia (Blazing Star). *Mentzelia lindleyi,* still known to many gardeners as *Bartonia aurea,* and so listed in seedsmen's catalogues, is a plant with striking golden-yellow flowers with showy stamens on 18-in. stems. It flowers from June to September. Young plants are quick to flower but open only when the sun shines. A sunny position and light soil are required.

Seeds should be sown in April or May where the plants are to flower. Seedlings are difficult to transplant.

Mignonette, see Reseda

Nasturtium, see Tropaeolum

Nemophila (Baby Blue Eyes). The California Bluebell, nemophila, bears a profusion of sky-blue flowers. If seeds are sown at intervals from mid-March to mid-May the plant can be had in bloom throughout the summer. This is an early-flowering annual content with ordinary garden soil and enjoying a cool, moist situation.

Nemophila insignis has large, gentian-blue, bell-shaped flowers, sometimes white centred. The young plant grows erect but becomes prostrate when spreading. There is a white form that

Top left: Nigella, or Love-in-a-Mist, an excellent annual for garden display and cutting
Bottom left: A mixture of the Virginian Stock, *Malcomia maritima*

Top right: The Sweet Pea Gertrude Tingay
Bottom right: Papaver nudicaule, the Iceland Poppy, is a perennial best grown as biennial (see p. 137) although it can also be treated as a half-hardy annual

associates happily with the azure blue species. *N. maculata* has delicately shaped white, purple-spotted flowers.

Seeds can be sown in March or April or in September where the plants are to flower.

Nicandra (Apple of Peru or Shoo Fly Plant). This plant is alleged to keep whitefly away, and any insect feeding on its sap quickly expires. I remain unconvinced about the truth of this story. The plant is robust and leafy and bears bell-shaped flowers followed by miniature apple fruits. It likes a sunny, open border and asks for no more than ordinary garden soil. Staking is usually necessary.

Nicandra physaloides, 3 ft., bears blue and white flowers from July to September.

Seeds should be sown in April.

Nigella (Love-in-a-Mist). This attractive annual is a favourite for cutting, with sky-blue flowers blessed with the lightest of feathery foliage. Any good garden soil is suitable for this plant, provided it is given an open, sunny position. The sky-blue Miss Jekyll, 18 in., still holds her place as one of the belles of the genus, but there are now Oxford blues, shades of rose pink and a white included in the delightful 15-in. Persian Jewels strain. These flower from June to September.

Sowings can be made in March or April or in September and the seed should be sown as thinly as possible.

Papaver (Annual Poppy). When the stems of these plants are cut a thick white juice exudes. They require plenty of sun and good garden soil.

Papaver commutatum has 1½-ft. stems and scarlet flowers with a black blotch at the base of the petals. The Carnation and Peony-flowered types, derived from *P. somniferum,* have their attractions but it is the Shirley Strain, 1½–2 ft., derived from our native field poppy, *P. rhoeas,* that is the pride of the family. The Shirley Poppies, single or densely double, rose, pink, red, blush or white, or any of the delicate bicolors that come in between, are captivating flowers the summer through.

All the above should be raised from March or April sowings made where the plants are to flower,

for the seedlings transplant poorly. Sowings of Shirley Poppies can also be made in September.

Phacelia. *Phacelia campanularia* is a much-loved, clear gentian-blue dwarf annual of 9 in. which flowers from June to September. It needs sun and a well-drained soil. There are other species, among them the 2-ft. *P. tanacetifolia,* with flower heads that slowly unfurl into clusters of lavender colour that are much to the taste of the bees. They all flower from July to September.

March, April and September sowings can be made.

Pincushion Flower, see Scabiosa

Poppy, Annual, see Papaver

Prince's Feather, see Amaranthus

Reseda (Mignonette). *Reseda odorata* is one of the most fragrant of annuals, with bold spikes of small, yellowish-white flowers that are pleasantly restful in a colour-dazzling border. This plant should be given a sunny position. It is unfussy about soil but has a preference for chalk and often survives the winter in a warm area.

Reseda odorata has produced numerous varieties, 1–1½ ft., some with deep yellow, gold and reddish heads, tapered or pyramidal, while Crimson Giant and red Goliath have immense spikes, deliciously scented, that arrive from June to September.

Sowings should be made in April or May where the plants are to flower.

Rose of Heaven, see Agrostemma

Sage, see Salvia

Salvia (Common Sage, primarily a herb). There are a number of hardy annual species and varieties in lavender, purple, pink and white that, although desirable, are too seldom grown. A sunny position and ordinary garden soil suits these plants.

Salvia horminum, known as Clary, has decorative purple-blue bracts and there are showy varieties such as Blue Beard, with spikes of blue bracts on 1½-ft. stems; Oxford Blue, 1½ ft.; Pink Sundae, 1½ ft. and Pink Lady, 15 in. All flower from July to September.

April sowing is advisable.

Saponaria. The pretty pink-flowered *Saponaria*

Top: Tidy-tips, *Layia elegans,* a sun lover with yellow, white-tipped flowers
Bottom: The Opium Poppy, *Papaver somniferum,* of which there are Peony- and Carnation-flowered strains

vaccaria, 2 ft., is useful for cutting and is satisfied with ordinary soil. The variety Pink Beauty is better than the species. It should be given a sunny position.

Seeds may be sown in March, April or May where the plants are to flower. September sowings can also be made.

Scabiosa (Scabious, Pincushion Flower). *Scabiosa atropurpurea,* the Sweet Scabious, has numerous single and double varieties, some 3 ft., with white, pink, red, maroon, pale mauve, blue and purple flowers. An especially fine variety is Black Prince with large, double, deep purple flowers, while the annual bee-hive-shaped scabious are well represented by the Cockade strain of almost conical form. Other varieties include the lavender-blue Blue Moon, Parma Violet and the scarlet Fire King, as well as the Tom Thumb dwarf strain with compact, medium-sized flowers from 1–1½ ft. All flower from July to September.

These plants may be treated as hardy or half-hardy annuals. If seed is sown in the autumn in boxes in a cold frame, the seedlings should be protected from frost and planted out in March or April. It is advisable to find the plants a sheltered position, otherwise staking may be necessary. Alternatively, seed may be sown in April where the plants are to flower.

Scabious, see Scabiosa

Silene (Catchfly). This old-fashioned annual is easily grown in light or sandy garden soil in a sunny border.

Silene pendula compacta is a neat, fragile dwarf with clusters of pink flowers and there are also crimson, ruby-red and white forms, as well as a double mixture. These will flower throughout the summer.

Sowings are made in March or April or in September to provide plants which will flower from late spring to mid-summer.

Shoo Fly Plant, see Nicandra

Sweet Alyssum, see Alyssum

Sweet Pea, see Lathyrus

Sweet Sultan, see Centaurea

Tassel Flower, see Emilia

Top: Blooms of the Cockade strain of the Sweet Scabious, *Scabiosa atropurpurea*
Bottom: The colourful semi-tall, double Nasturtium, *Tropaeolum* Golden Gleam

Tidy Tips, see Layia

Toadflax, see Linaria

Tropaeolum (Nasturtium). The nasturtium is the most widely grown annual we possess. The plants with golden, orange, scarlet, salmon and cherry-rose flowers make large bushes and throw out short runners.

Nasturtiums enjoy the sunshine and thrive in the poorest of soils. Regular dead-heading is essential if the plants are to flower generously for a long period.

Tropaeolum majus is a climbing species and it is from this plant that the majority of garden nasturtiums have been derived, including the tall climbing varieties, the semi-tall Gleam and the dwarf or Tom Thumb nasturtiums, the sweet-scented semi-doubles and the dwarf doubles.

Tropaeolum peltophorum, Lobb's Climbing Nasturtium, with orange-red flowers, has hairy stems and small foliage. Garden varieties descended from this species include bright red Spitfire and scarlet Lucifer.

T. peregrinum is the Canary Creeper or Canary Flower, with delightfully fringed flowers and pale green foliage. It is often listed by seedsmen under its former name, *T. canariense*. It is a self-climber that will scale a 12-ft. trellis in one season. All flower from July to September or later, if the weather is kind.

Sowings can be made in April or May.

Viper's Bugloss, see Echium

Virginian Stock, see Malcomia

Viscaria. This is another attractive annual of 12–15 in., but some dwarf mixtures of 6 in. are offered by seedsmen. Certain named varieties are also available. The colour range includes red, pink, shades of blue and white, and their flowering period is June to October. Ordinary garden soil and a sunny position will suit this plant. To be botanically correct, the viscarias should be listed under the genus *Lychnis* but they will always be found in seedsmen's catalogues under the former heading.

Seeds should be sown in March or April.

Woodruff, see Asperula

Cultivation of Half-hardy Annuals

This group of plants needs warmer conditions than can be provided in British gardens during the early stages of their growth cycle, assuming they are wanted to flower at about the same time as the hardy annuals. It should be noted, however, that many of them can be sown in the open ground from late May to early June when the soil has warmed up, but they will flower much later.

Half-hardy annuals are normally raised from sowings made in pots or boxes in a warm greenhouse or frame from early February until the end of April. However, too much heat should be avoided and a mean temperature of 10°C. (50°F.) suits the majority of these plants better than 16°C. (60°F.). The novice should beware of the temperature creeping up during the daytime–this can be regulated by ventilation–but at night it can be allowed to fall to a minimum of 7°C. (45°F.).

Using Cloches

Those gardeners who do not possess a greenhouse but have a few cloches and the know-how, can raise half-hardy annuals of the highest standard as robust as and perhaps earlier in the season than their better-equipped competitors.

Cloches of the 'barn' type with glass ends should be placed in position where the seeds are to be sown in late March and early April, about a week to ten days before sowing, in order to warm up the soil. This will also dry it out and it may be necessary to water before sowing so that the soil is sufficiently moist to encourage germination. In warmer parts of the country it will be possible to sow the seed from late March onwards and a couple of weeks later in cooler areas. By mid-May it should be possible to remove the cloches but if frosts are forecast then they must be replaced during the vulnerable night hours.

Suitable Composts

Boxes in which annual seedlings are to be raised must be hospital clean with well-spaced drainage holes and contain a compost of good loam to which has been added well-decayed manure (if available), leafmould and sand so that the mixture is rich and porous. John Innes Seed Compost will serve for the pricking out of the majority of seedlings, the ingredients being as follows: 2 parts by bulk sterilised loam, 1 part granulated peat and 1 part of coarse sand, plus $1\frac{1}{2}$ oz. of superphosphate of lime and $\frac{3}{4}$ oz. of ground chalk or limestone per bushel.

Large seeds and robust plants needing stronger fare should be treated to John Innes Potting Compost which consists of 7 parts by bulk of sifted sterilised loam, 3 parts granulated peat and 2 parts of coarse sand, plus 4 oz. of John Innes Base Fertiliser and $\frac{3}{4}$ oz. ground chalk or limestone per bushel. The advantage of these John Innes composts is that they are correctly balanced and sterilised. Buying from the sundriesman saves a lot of time and saucepan trouble. Sterilising soil in the kitchen has, to my knowledge, led to many an argument between cook and gardener!

Later Treatment

The seedlings should be grown on under glass until the spring. Then, after careful hardening off, they can be planted out at the end of May or the beginning of June, depending on the weather.

Half-hardy annuals call for more attention and care than hardy annuals and success depends on hardening them off and acclimatising them without checking their growth. I am often asked whether the work involved is justified. Personally, I am sure that it is. After all, they are the most interesting, varied and rewarding group with many beauties among them, and once established they flower on until killed by frost.

It will be noticed that I have juggled the heliotrope and the pelargonium (geranium), both half-hardy perennials, into the half-hardy annuals (see pp. 118 and 122 respectively) as no book on summer flowers should be without them.

Attractive Half-hardy Annuals

Ageratum (Floss Flower). This small perennial with blue, fluffy heads seldom survives the frost. It is an excellent groundwork bedding plant for the front of the border, and is now to be had in perhaps less effective pink and white varieties. They flower from July until autumn.

This dwarf plant (between 4 and 9 in., although there is a variety of 1½ ft. called Tall Blue) is happy in a warm sunny position and thrives on ordinary soil. Dwarf varieties include Little Blue Star, Blue Mink and Dwarf Mauve.

Sowings should be made in March and the seedlings planted out in May.

Alonsoa (The Mask Flower). With sprays of small schizanthus-like flowers of brilliant scarlet, this plant enjoys a sunny situation and rich fare. It benefits by being pinched back when young to encourage a bushy habit.

Alonsoa warscewiczii, 1½ ft., has bright scarlet flowers and is particularly bright and showy. *A. mutisii,* a delicate pink form, is a compact dwarf of 9–12 in. These flower from July to October.

Late March sowings should be made under glass, or outdoor sowing at the end of April or in May.

Amaranthus (Joseph's Coat). I have already sung the praises of the amaranthus which can be grown as hardy annuals (see p. 96, Love-Lies-Bleeding and Prince's Feather), and am now concerned with the half-hardy kinds with showy foliage and spikes of red flowers—*Amaranthus tricolor* and its varieties. These bear the common name of Joseph's Coat and the species itself, about 1½ ft., has showy variegated foliage of purplish red and yellow, marked with green at the tip. The variety *splendens,* 1 ft., is even more strongly coloured, and a variety introduced from Japan, Shoojoy, 3 ft., is an exciting subject with leaves of purple, carmine and scarlet. Molton Fire, 1½ ft., is another spectacular variety with purple, bronze and red leaves. All these provide a gay show from July to September.

Seeds should be sown in March and germinated in a temperature of 16°C. (60°F.). The young plants which result can be planted out in May.

Anagallis (The Pimpernel). This plant, to be effective, should be mass planted at the front of the border. Ordinary soil and a sunny situation suits it well, provided the border is well drained.

Anagallis linifolia (syn. *A. grandiflora*) with lovely blue flowers on 6-in. stems from July to September, is the most desirable member of the genus, but there are also red and rosy kinds and mixtures of colours can be obtained.

Antirrhinum (Snapdragon). The showy antirrhinums need no introduction to the gardener. The modern garden varieties are derived from *Antirrhinum majus,* a perennial plant, but they are grown as half-hardy annuals from sowings made in February or March under glass–or in late summer if spring-flowering plants are desired.

There are tall, intermediate or semi-dwarf and dwarf varieties of *A. majus* in lovely colours from orange, crimson, pink, apricot and yellow to mauve and white. These are of 2–4 ft., 1½ ft., and 9–10 in. in height respectively.

These plants love the sunshine, but are vulnerable to rust if planted in excessively dry situations. Rust-resistant varieties should be grown where the disease persists. If the dead flower heads are removed regularly, flowering will be continuous until the autumn.

New varieties and strains of F_1 hybrids are introduced every year. The doubles (2 ft.), the tubular penstemon-flowered (1½ ft.), the hyacinth-flowered (1¼ ft.), the American tetraploids that have giant crested spikes of bloom (2–2½ ft.), and the trumpet-shaped Bright Butterflies all have their followers.

I have referred above to the two periods when seed can be sown under glass. Seedlings from August sowings should be overwintered in a cold frame and planted out in April or May. Seedlings from February or March sowings, made in gentle heat, may be planted out in May, after hardening off. (Plants raised in this way will flower from June to October.)

Arctotis. This brilliant, prolific, daisy-flowered South African plant is quick to mature and flower but is a tender subject. The colour range of the flower has been extended from cream to orange, red, crimson and purple with zones of contrasting colours. The arctotis are sun lovers and they need a well-drained, rather dry position.

Arctotis grandis, with long-stemmed, pearl-white flowers and mauve centres circled with a narrow golden band, is an elegant, interesting species, 1½–2 ft., from which a delightful range of hybrids have been bred. These have a lovely colour range including numerous pastel shades, often possessing contrasting zones of orange and a striking blue disc.

Something must be said, too, about Sutton's Special Hybrids, among the most exciting half-hardy introductions of the last decade. The plants are bushy and vigorous, only 9 in. high and their flowers come in seven shades–ivory, cream, yellow, orange, red, crimson and wine–with contrasting basal markings.

Sowings should be made in March in gentle heat and the seedlings should be planted out in May, after hardening off.

Balsam, see Impatiens

Begonia. The ever-blooming bedding begonia and the large-flowered tuberous begonia, both flowering from June to October, are half-hardy perennials but I am including them here as they are best raised as half-hardy annuals. Begonias prefer a rather moist soil and a cool semi-shaded position. If grown in a sunny border they should be planted in soil containing peat or leafmould to hold the moisture.

The Semperflorens type of begonia flowers continuously from July to October and is capable of surviving a wet summer or an August drought. These extremely valuable small bedding plants have flowers of white, pink, rose and orange-scarlet, and may be between 4 in. and 12 in. in height. The Organdy mixture of F_1 hybrids,

4–6 in., are especially attractive with their fine colour range and are splendid bedding plants. Some have attractive red or purplish foliage.

The Multiflora type are attractive with a profusion of double, semi-double or single flowers, from June onwards. They are excellent for growing in window-boxes and for bedding out. They can be bought as tubers or may be grown from seed. Mrs. Helen Harmes is an outstanding golden-yellow and Tasso a fine dark scarlet double.

The tuberous-rooted begonias, both single and double, have very large blooms, a long flowering season, and come in a wide range of colours. The magnificent flower heads have, however, an unfortunate habit of dropping off following excessive changes in temperature, as when hot days follow cold nights.

Seeds should be sown in January or February in a steady temperature of 16° to 18°C. (60° to 65°F.). Begonia seed is often extremely small and is better lightly pressed into the compost than covered with soil. The seedlings which result should be pricked out into pots when large enough to handle and later, after careful hardening off, bedded out in early June when all danger of frost has past. The Multiflora type can be raised from seed and will produce tubers which can be used again in subsequent years after winter storing. The same applies to the tuberous-rooted type.

Bells of Ireland, see Molucella

Blanket Flower, see Gaillardia

Blue Daisy, see Felicia

Blue Marguerite, see Felicia

Brachycome (Swan River Daisy). The dwarf, branching *Brachycome iberidifolia,* 1½ ft., is an Australian annual which is useful for filling a gap in the front of the border or will serve as an edging plant. The attractive daisy-like flowers are in lavender, blue, purple, pink and white. This plant succeeds in a dry, sunny situation.

Many forms of *B. iberidifolia* are available, some only 9 in. in height. Purple Splendour, 8 in., is an attractive new variety which will flower from June to October.

Seeds can be sown under glass in March to provide plants for planting out in May, or sowings can be made in the open ground in April, but flowering will then, inevitably, be considerably later.

Callistephus (China Aster). The decorative China Asters, derived from *Callistephus chinensis,* vary tremendously these days and there are singles, double, ray-petalled, ostrich-plumed, incurved, anemone-flowered, chrysanthemum-flowered, pompons, powder puffs, giants and lilliputs to choose from. The flower range is equally wide: there are whites, primroses, pinks, scarlets, mauves, blues and purples galore in August and September.

Asters thrive in rich soil and will tolerate semi-shade while preferring a sunny site. Greenfly have a liking for them and action should be taken to control this pest immediately its presence is detected.

Gardeners like myself who have a bias towards single flowers will favour the single Marguerite or Sinensis type with long stiff stems: they are to be had in a large range of colours and shades. The variety Apple Blossom makes particularly attractive cut flowers, 1½ ft.

Sowings can be made in March or April under glass, the seedlings being planted out in rich loam in May, after hardening off. Damping off can be troublesome at the seedling stage and should be countered by watering the boxes with Cheshunt Compound. Seed may also be sown in the open in late April or early May, the seedlings being thinned out as soon as they are large enough to handle.

Castor Oil Plant, see Ricinus

Celosia (Cockscomb). The Cockscombs are feathered or crested, in gay shades of orange, scarlet, bronze, crimson, gold, creamy white and pink, and it is the feathered sorts which can be grown outdoors when all danger of frost has passed. The Lilliput strain, 1 ft., is useful for this purpose. The Cockscombs have their admirers, but they are an acquired taste.

Seed is best sown from March onwards under glass. When seedlings have formed four leaves they should be given individual pots and it is important to keep the plants close to the glass. Daily syringing will be found helpful. Young plants can be put outdoors in late May or early in June.

Cherry Pie, see Heliotropium

China Aster, see Callistephus

Cleome (Spider Flower). With big clusters of pink spider-like flowers that have telling stamens, *Cleome spinosa* is a handsome plant for the middle of the border. It demands a warm position and good soil and should not be allowed to go dry.

The variety Rose Queen bears large, apple-pink flower spikes for months on end and is one of the best tall annuals, growing to 3 ft.

Seeds should be sown in March in gentle heat, and the young plants planted out in a warm position in May.

Cobaea. The Cup-and-Saucer Plant or Cathedral Bells, the Mexican *Cobaea scandens* is a vigorous climber with tendrils that assist the plant in rapidly covering a trellis or fence with thin growth up to a height of 10 ft. The bell flowers are fascinating with protruding stamens and petals that turn from green to violet.

This is a tender perennial grown as a half-hardy annual, and it thrives in a sheltered position in partial shade. It is an extremely decorative climber, and a white form is also available.

Sowings should be made under glass in March in a temperature of 16° to 21°C. (60° to 70°F.) and the young plants may be put out in June.

Cockscomb, see Celosia

Cone Flower, see Rudbeckia

Cosmea, see Cosmos

Cosmos (Cosmea). The large, single, broad-petalled flowers of the Mexican Cosmeas are borne on long, wiry stems. The flat faces are in white, pink, crimson and scarlet. The latest introductions have zones of contrasting colour, and the foliage is finely cut and fern-like. The Cosmeas are easy-going plants and they enjoy the sun.

Varieties of *Cosmos bipinnatus* in crimson, pink,

rose and white are ideal for the back of the annual border and may be treated as hardy annuals in warm parts of the country. These grow up to 4 ft. The Sensation strain, excellent for cutting, includes attractive colours, and mention must be made of *C. sulphureus* and its varieties, among them highly successful orange-red, semi-double Sunset, 3 ft., that has been awarded a gold medal in the All-America Trials. Flowers arrive freely from July to October.

Seeds should be sown under glass in March to provide plants for planting out in May.

Cucurbita (Gourds). The showy climbing ornamental gourds have their attraction in the garden, after which the fruits may be cut and used for decoration in the house. *Cucurbita maxima, C. pepo* and *C. moschata* and their varieties are all half-hardy annuals useful for this purpose. They include the Pumpkins, Marrows and Squashes, while seeds of various mixtures are offered with fruit in the shape of apples, pears, oranges, gooseberries, bottles, eggs and so on. The gourd list also includes the Fig-leaf, Calabash, Caveman's Club, Powderhorn, Siphon and Turk's

Turban types. There are colours and shapes for all tastes.

Once the fruits have ripened they may be cut and dried. Some gardeners make a small circular incision in the skin in which a teaspoon can be inserted so that the soft inside matter of the fruit can be removed before varnishing. The circular piece may then be replaced and disguised with a little paint.

Seeds should be sown in trays or individual pots under glass in gentle heat in April; after hardening off, the resulting seedlings may be planted out in early June.

Everlasting Flower, see Helichrysum

Felicia (The Kingfisher Daisy, Blue Daisy, Blue Marguerite). The Kingfisher Daisy, *Felicia bergeriana,* is a showy annual when the sun shines, its brilliant blue flowers possessing golden centres. A South African sun lover of 4–6 in., it makes a charming pot plant for the greenhouse as well as a splendid edging plant. The half-hardy perennial species, *F. amelloides,* the Blue Daisy or Blue Marguerite, with sky-blue flowers, can also be grown as a half-hardy annual.

Bottom left: The familiar handsome flowers and ferny foliage of cosmos, the Cosmea
Bottom right: The striking ornamental Maize, *Zea mays japonica,* with white striped foliage

Sow seeds in March to provide plants for setting out in late May or early June. Alternatively, in the case of *F. bergeriana,* sow seed outdoors in late April or May.

Floss Flower, see Ageratum

Gaillardia (Blanket Flower). *Gaillardia pulchella* and its hybrids, single and double, are the half-hardy annual members of this genus, with yellow, crimson, orange-red and copper-scarlet flowers. The ball-shaped Lollipop strain in lemon, raspberry red and some red or yellow tipped, are floriferous, compact and weather resistant, and grow to 1 ft. The slightly taller, double-flowered Lorenziana strain is popular with its range of yellow, orange and red shades. All flower from July to September making a colourful display in the border.

Sowings should be made in March to provide plants for setting out in May.

Gazania. These trailing plants with large, brilliant orange, orange-red or cream daisy flowers are marked with attractive dark or black zones. The pink and red hybrids are more recent arrivals and the colour range is being constantly extended.

The flowers have an enchanting way of flinging themselves open to the sun.

These plants demand warmth and sunshine, and although prepared to grow in the poorest of soils, they respond generously to a loam and peat mixture. Plants brought inside for the winter and planted out again in late spring often give a fine performance in the second summer, for they are half-hardy perennials, flowering in the first year if sown early enough (in March, under glass, planting the young plants out in late May or early June).

Geranium, see Pelargonium

Gourds, see Cucurbita

Grasses (Ornamental kinds, see also p. 103). The following ornamental grasses are best grown as half-hardy annuals: *Milium effusum aureum* (Bowles' Golden Grass), *Pennisetum longistylum* (syn. *P. villosum*), with graceful feathery plumes, and *Setaria glauca*. These grasses are all much in demand by flower arrangers. The white-striped *Zea mays gracillima variegata,* and *Z. m. japonica* and *Z. m. japonica quadricolor,* striped white, yellow and rose, have a sub-tropical look.

Top: Bells of Ireland, *Molucella Laevis*, a flower much in demand for flower arranging
Bottom: Helichrysums, Everlasting Flowers, are plants for sunny positions. The bracts retain their colour for long periods

Sowings should be made in March in heat, to produce young plants to put out in late May or early June.

Helichrysum (Everlasting Flower, see also p. 64). The half-hardy annuals of this genus include *H. bracteatum monstrosum* (double everlasting), 2–3 ft., in a wide range of colours–orange, yellow, crimson, pink and white–and a dwarf form, 1½ ft. with an equally good colour spread. These flower from July to September.

Seeds should be sown in March in gentle heat and the young plants put out at the beginning of May. They can also be treated as hardy annuals, sowing seeds outdoors in April.

Heliotrope, see Heliotropium

Heliotropium (Heliotrope, Cherry Pie). This mauve and purple Peruvian plant is by no means colourful, but the large flower trusses are deliciously scented. Varieties with flowers of white and shades of carmine are available but little seen. This is a tender perennial generally treated as a half-hardy annual, for it will flower the first year from seed. Heliotropes require ordinary good soil and a sunny position; they are vulnerable to frost.

Heliotropium peruvianum is the progenitor of the more colourful modern garden strains, many of which unfortunately have little or no scent. The Regale hybrids, 1½–2 ft., are much grown and the violet-purple Marine, 2 ft. A well-scented rather than a decorative variety should be the gardener's choice. The flowering period is June to September.

Seeds should be sown in February or March in gentle heat, the young plants being put out in the garden in early June.

Hop, see Humulus

Humulus (Hop). This is a perennial climbing plant grown as an annual. *Humulus japonicus*, the Japanese Hop, has a variegated variety, *variegatus*, which makes a useful screening plant with its green and white foliage. It will grow to 8–10 ft., and is an excellent leafy climber for camouflaging an eye-sore.

Seeds should be sown ⅛ in. deep in pots of good soil in a cool or heated greenhouse in April, the young plants being put outdoors in May or

June. Ordinary good soil and the support of a sunny or shady wall, trellis or tree stump suits the hop.

Impatiens (Balsam). The genus *Impatiens* includes annuals and half-hardy perennials, both of which can be grown as half-hardy annuals. Patient Lucy, the popular office plant, belongs to this genus. Impatiens is now becoming a favourite bedding plant, having been greatly improved in colour and habit by the plant breeders. It is an unfussy subject but enjoys a syringing and regular watering during drought.

Impatiens balsamina, 2 ft., with flowers in white, red, blue and yellow, has resulted in numerous forms, the double varieties with blooms like camellias, and *I. holstii* presents hybrids of about 1 ft. in a good colour range. A new F_1 hybrid is the gay General Guisan, 5–10 in. tall with red and white flowers. Another recent introduction is the 6-in. Imp strain in numerous attractive colours. The dwarf Tom Thumb strain, 10 in., also deserves consideration.

Seeds should be sown in March in a temperature of 16°C. (60°F.) and later the seedlings treated to individual pots. They can then be planted out in late May or early June with the minimum of disturbance.

Ipomoea (Morning Glory). *Ipomoea tricolor* is the beautiful and by no means menacing relation of the invasive Bindweed. It is a climber best known for its outstanding azure-blue variety, Heavenly Blue. This plant must be given a trellis or support up which to climb, and a warm, sunny position protected from the wind. It enjoys a light, rich soil. There are double-flowered varieties and blooms in white, wine red, pink and scarlet, accompanied by heart-shaped leaves. A bicolor with an up-to-the-minute name is Flying Saucers, white and bright blue. The flowers last from July to October.

Seeds should be sown in March under glass; germination may be erratic and can be assisted by either chipping the seed or soaking it in warm water for 24 hours before sowing. Planting out should be delayed until a mild spell in June.

Joseph's Coat, see Amaranthus
Kingfisher Daisy, see Felicia
Kochia (The Summer Cypress). This foliage plant has light green leaves which turn to brilliant carmine in autumn. The unimportant scarlet flowers are clustered in the leaf axils. Kochias thrive in a light soil in a sunny position.

K. scoparia trichophla is the variety usually grown. It makes a neat little bush about 2 ft. high and 1 ft. across. The variety *K. childsii* also colours splendidly in the autumn.

Seeds should be sown in April and the plants which result set out in May or early June. Alternatively, an outdoor sowing can be made in May.

Limonium (Statice, Sea Lavender). There is now an array of everlasting flowers in pastel shades that make delightful winter bouquets. The yellow-flowered *Limonium bonduellii,* a good half-hardy perennial species, and the *sinuatum* Art Shades, 1½ ft., now available in a wonderful range of pastel colours, are best treated as half-hardy annuals and grown in a sunny position. The flowers are borne from August to October. These plants are often found in seedsmen's catalogues listed under their former name, Statice.

Sowings should be made in February or March under glass, the seedlings being pricked out into boxes and planted in the garden in May. The seeds are held in the dried flower heads and these should be pressed into the soil and only lightly covered. Each flower cluster is estimated to hold two seeds. Seedlings are transplantable.

Livingstone Daisy, see Mesembryanthemum
Lobelia. The garden varieties, 4–6 in., so much seen in bedding schemes, are mostly derived from the South African *Lobelia erinus*. The gay blue flowers often regimented in line formation are far more effective when planted in blocks. Lobelias enjoy a rich, light and well-drained soil. Young plants should be pinched back at an early stage to keep them bushy.

There are a host of excellent garden varieties, 4–6 in. in height. Cambridge Blue is renowned. Crystal Palace, an intense dark blue, has attractive bronze foliage; Snowball, white dwarf; Mrs.

The Morning Glory, *Ipomoea tricolor*, the annual
climber that gives an exciting daily performance
in summer sunshine

Clibran Improved, deep blue with a white eye;
Prima Donna, a distinctive wine colour;
Rosamund, carmine-red with a white eye–all
have their charms. There is, too, the trailing
Sapphire, blue with a white eye, and Blue
Cascade.

Seeds should be sown in February or March in
a temperature of 16°C. (60°F.). They should be
sown as thinly as possible and then covered very
lightly with soil. Alternatively, an autumn sowing
can be made and the young seedlings over-
wintered under glass should robust plants be
wanted for early summer flowering. The spring
sowing will provide flowers from July to October.

Marigold, see Tagetes

Mask Flower, see Alonsoa

Matthiola (Stock, see also p. 136). The Beauty of
Nice or Mammoth Stocks, 1½ to 2 ft., are a free-
flowering strain including many attractive colours,
the lovely Violette de Parma and yellow to pink
and rose shades, purple, blue, lavender and
white. They, and the Giant Imperials, Giant
Perfection, and the Ten-Week Stocks are best
raised as half-hardy annuals. Stocks enjoy a good
soil and a taste of mortar rubble.

Sowings should be made in March in gentle
heat. It should be remembered that seedlings
grown in too close an atmosphere are quick to
become drawn and leggy. Plant out in late May
or early June after hardening off.

Mesembryanthemum (Livingstone Daisy).
Mesembryanthemum criniflorum, a plant of spreading habit bearing a host of daisy-like flowers in
dazzling orange, carmine, red and pastel shades,
and white flowers edged or tinted with pink,
buff or magenta. These low-growing plants
thrive in a dry, sunny position and appreciate a
taste of mortar rubble in the soil. They are unsurpassed in brilliance in seaside gardens. A
surprisingly good performance is given by plants
on the poorest of soils in a sun-baked spot.
Mesembryanthemum tricolor, 3 in., deep rose and
white, is an elegant species and a better mixer than
many. They flower from July to September.

Seeds should be sown under glass in a temperature of 16°C. (60°F.) in March or April, and the
resulting seedlings later hardened off in a cold
frame and planted out in May. Alternatively, an
outdoor sowing can be made in April or May but
the flowers will not, of course, appear until much
later than those of plants raised from earlier sowings under glass.

Mexican Sunflower, see Tithonia

Mimulus (Monkey Flower). The numerous
perennial mimulus are much grown as annuals
and are splendid plants for a sheltered position in a
rather damp soil. The trumpet-shaped flowers
have a distinctive appearance and strains offered
by seedsmen include a delightful colour range.
Many have flowers attractively blotched and
otherwise marked and the colours include orange,
scarlet, yellow, rose, pink, salmon and buff.

Seeds should be sown in March and planting
out should be done either in late May or early June
during a mild spell.

Molucella (Bells of Ireland, Shell Flower). This
highly decorative, half-hardy annual can be cut
and stored as an everlasting flower. The white
flowers are borne in whorls up the stems, and each
flower is framed in a pale sea-green calyx. The
flower arrangers usually remove the foliage
leaving the calyces to ripen and turn to a cream-
ivory colour. *Molucella laevis,* the 2-ft. species
usually grown, is a great favourite in America.

Seeds are sown in late March or April in a
temperature of around 16° to 18°C. (60° to
65°F.) and the young plants put out in late May or
early June.

Monarch of the Veldt, see Venidium

Monkey Flower, see Mimulus

Morning Glory, see Ipomoea

Nemesia. Nemesias are quick growers which
need a little extra care. The gardener must beware
of the plants becoming leggy and showing bud
and flower before planting out time. For this
reason seed is better sown in late rather than
early March, particular care being taken to
harden off the seedlings correctly. Nemesias
require a rich, moist soil, a sunny position and
plenty of elbow room.

Top: The F₁ hybrid petunias possess beauty, vigour
and uniformity of colour and habit. F₁ Resisto Mixed
is shown above
Bottom: The handsome Caster Oil Plant,
Ricinus communis gibsonii, with bronze leaves

Sutton's large-flowered strain, growing to 12 in.,
includes such separate colours as scarlet, bronze
and pink shades, orange, rose-pink, cherry red,
yellow and white (Suttons introduced nemesias
from South Africa 77 years ago). Another popular
variety is Blue Gem, 9 in.; Fire King, of the same
height, is an eye-catching crimson-scarlet, while
the dwarf Triumph strain also presents a wealth
of small blooms. The flowering time for the
nemesias is July to September.

Seeds should be sown in late March or April in
a temperature of 16° to 18°C. (60° to 65°F.); the
resulting seedlings grown on and hardened off
without a check, may be planted out in May or
early June.

Nicotiana (Tobacco Plant). *Nicotiana affinis* (or,
to be more correct, *N. alata* var. *grandiflora*) is the
progenitor of present-day ornamental Tobacco
Plants. For many years the flowers of these
delightfully scented plants partially closed during
the day and only opened at night to scent the air
with their fragrance. The modern varieties remain open during the day, but alas have lost
nearly all their fragrance. Among these are the
white-flowered Daylight, 1½ ft., Dwarf White
Bedder, 15 in., the Sensation Mixed Strain, 2½ ft.,
and the deep red novelty Idol, 10 in.

The unusual and delightful variety Lime Green,
1½ ft., has been a best-seller for some years and
its lovely greenish-yellow flowers are a break-
through in colour. Crimson King, 2½ ft., a cross
between *affinis* and the hybrid *sanderae*, is another
example of the development in this genus, and
the mixed *sanderae* hybrids, 2½ ft., include crimson,
rose, mauve and white flowers.

Sowings should be made in February or March
in gentle heat and the young plants hardened off
and put out in May or early June.

Pelargonium (Geranium). It might seem surprising to find the Geranium, the V.I.P. of the
window-box and summer bedding, in a chapter
on half-hardy annuals, but as seed of F₁ hybrids
are freely on offer by seedsmen they now fall
neatly into this category.

The Carefree F₁ hybrids from America are now

available in bright pink, scarlet, deep salmon and white. All being well they make $1\frac{1}{2}$-ft. tall plants and can be relied upon to come true from seed.

Seeds of the Carefree strain should be sown in January or February and young plants put out in early June, when all danger of frost has past.

Petunia. The petunias with their broad and open, long, funnel-shaped flowers in white, mauve, purple, pink and crimson, are among the finest of half-hardy annuals we possess. They require a hot, fine summer to be seen at their best and prefer a light, rich soil and sunny position.

The F_1 hybrids lead nowadays because of their beauty, vigour, uniformity of colour and habit.

There are the large-flowered single and double Grandifloras, 9–12 in., which produce immense blooms with great frequency; the low-growing single Multifloras, 6–9 in., which include beauties such as Sugar Plum, the Satin varieties and exciting bicolors; and the double Multifloras, 12–15 in., with frilled and carnation-like double flowers. These last, led by the rose and white Cherry Tart, put up a magnificent show in a fine summer.

In addition to the F_1 hybrids there are also the cheaper bedding varieties which also provide a colourful display.

Seed should be sown in March in boxes of light compost. The small seed must be sown as thinly as possible and sprinkled afterwards with a suspicion of soil. The boxes should then be covered with glass or brown paper to encourage germination. The resulting seedlings may be pricked out when the second pair of true leaves has appeared and grown on and gradually hardened off until the end of May or beginning of June, when they can be planted out during a mild spell. Care must be taken during these early stages not to overwater.

Sowing too early is a common mistake with the result that the gardener has to hold back his young plants in boxes, even if overcrowded, before daring to plant them out. This often results in a check to growth.

Phlox. The annual phlox, varieties derived from *Phlox drummondii,* bear flowers in a wonderful range of colours: pink, rose, salmon, crimson, mauve, blue, purple and white, many with contrasting eyes. There are two main types, the Grandiflora (with large, rounded flowers borne in close terminal clusters) and the dwarf Nana Compacta (which make small plants smothered in round or star-shaped flowers). The phlox enjoys a rich soil capable of retaining moisture and a sunny position, and flowers from July to September.

The large-flowered group (about 1 ft.) are apt to be straggly and may need pegging down, but the dwarfs are models of tidiness. The dwarf Beauty strain (6 in.) and the robust Twinkle strain (6–8 in.) with star-like flowers are valuable bedders.

Seeds should be sown under glass in early March, the resulting seedlings pricked off into boxes as soon as they are large enough to handle and the young plants planted out in late May or June.

Pimpernel, see Anagallis

Portulaca. This low-growing, spreading plant with a profusion of orange-scarlet, rosy-purple, yellow or white flowers is an excellent subject for a dry bank. It should be given a light, rich, rather dry soil and revels in the sun.

Portulaca grandiflora is the strain usually grown, bearing single flowers in rose, pink, orange-scarlet, purple, yellow and white. Seedsmen offer a double mixture from which a high percentage of plants come true. Their height is about 6 in. and they flower from July to September.

Seed can be grown under glass in March, but as this plant resents transplanting a late April or early May sowing made outdoors where the plant is to flower is advised.

Ricinus (Castor Oil Plant). This half-hardy herb is a handsome foliage plant with bronze, purple or green leaves and insignificant flowers. The seeds are poisonous if eaten. It is happy in ordinary soil in a sunny border.

Ricinus communis cambodgensis, 5 ft., a plant of character, is decorative in the border with stems

Left: A selection of summer bedding plants—salvias, marigolds, selections of *Phlox drummondii,* alyssum and lobelia
Below right: Portulacas, low-growing, colourful plants and excellent, among other places, for a dry bank

and leaves of black-purple. *R. c. gibsonii,* 4–5 ft., has dark green stems and bronze foliage; *R c. sanguineus,* 5 ft., is a dramatic plant with reddish-purple foliage; and *R. c. zanzibarensis,* 6–8 ft., has striking bright green leaves of very large size with distinct midribs.

Seeds should be sown in March under glass in a temperature of 16°C. (60°F.). They should be steeped for a few hours in tepid water before sowing. When the seedlings are large enough to handle, they should be potted up individually. After being carefully hardened off they may be planted out in June.

Rudbeckia (Cone Flower). The annual rudbeckias thrive in dry soil and full sun. The Giant Tetraploid Hybrids (Gloriosa Daisies), $2\frac{1}{2}$–3 ft., with flowers up to 7 in. across in such colours as bronze, mahogany red, yellow and chestnut shades are spectacular border plants and excellent for cutting. The golden-yellow Double Gloriosa Daisy, with double or semi-double flowers, 3 ft.; bronze and chestnut Bambi, 1 ft.; and the yellow Sputnik, $1\frac{1}{2}$ ft., are all good border plants. All these flower from July to September.

If the bottom inch of the flower stems is immersed in boiling water for 30 minutes after cutting the flowers will last longer.

Seeds should be sown under glass in March, and the seedlings pricked off when large enough to handle and, after hardening off, be planted out in May. Alternatively, seeds may be sown in the open ground in summer to provide flowering plants earlier than usual in the following summer.

Sage, see Salvia

Salpiglossis. Salpiglossis have rich-looking tubular flowers of velvet texture in brilliant colourings—cream, gold, yellow, rose and crimson with gold veining, or blue, violet and purple, pencilled gold. These glorious flowers must be given a sheltered and sunny position and a well-drained, rich, light soil. They should be watered during periods of drought and treated to occasional mild doses of stimulant.

Salpiglossis sinuata, the branching Scalloped Tube Tongue, with large velvet flowers, is the

parent of many garden varieties. The new Splash hybrids, 2 ft., with a good colour range, have a new vigour and are free flowering, which is very welcome. *S. superbissima* (the Emperor strain), 2 ft., has very large flowers, while Sutton's Triumph, $2\frac{1}{2}$ ft., provides some of the brightest blooms. The flowering period is from July to September.

Seed should be sown under glass in February or March, keeping the temperature at around 13°C. (55°F.) until May when the plants should be placed in a cold frame to harden off. These are not easy plants to rear successfully. They are best grown in John Innes compost and watering must be carried out with care. Seedlings are transplantable and young plants should be put out in the garden during a warm spell in June. Seed may also be sown outdoors in late April or early May.

Salvia (Sage). The Scarlet Sage from Mexico, *Salvia splendens,* is widely grown as a bedding plant although its strident scarlet spires sometimes fall foul of next door neighbours in the border. However, there are purple and blue salvias that are easy to place. Ordinary, good, well-drained soil suits this plant and it gives a fine performance in a warm, sunny summer.

Salvia splendens includes a number of exciting scarlets, among them the very successful Blaze of Fire, 1 ft., and Firebird, 1½ ft. Besides the dazzling reds there is the very desirable *S. farinacea* Blue Bedder, 2½ ft., and the gentian-blue *S. patens,* 2 ft. The flowering period is from July to September.

Sowings should be made under glass in January or February. The seedlings should be potted up separately and later, after hardening off, the young plants can be put out in June.

Sea Lavender, see Limonium

Shell Flower, see Molucella

Snapdragon, see Antirrhinum

Spider Flower, see Cleome

Statice, see Limonium

Stock, see Matthiola

Summer Cypress, see Kochia

Swan River Daisy, see Brachycome

Tagetes (Marigold). The giant-flowered African Marigolds should perhaps head the marigold list. The modern F_1 hybrids carry immense double flowers of uniform colour and habit, and there are primrose, yellow, gold, glowing orange and red shades. They vary in height from 2–3 ft. The Climax strain and the Crackerjacks should especially be mentioned. The Jubilee F_1 hybrid strain is referred to as a hedge-type marigold because the foliage is so dense, providing a 2-ft. barrier. The large double blooms rise above the foliage. This carnation-flowered type and the chrysanthemum-flowered mixtures with shaggy and less formal flower heads are fine plants. But of all the marigolds, it is the dwarf French kinds that are the most outstanding: they are the showiest of all the half-hardy bedders. *Tagetes patula* is the progenitor of these small plants and it is interesting to note that research is now being carried out to discover whether the powerful excretions of the tagetes might be of value as a weedkiller against such troublemakers as the elder, convolvulus or couch grass.

This is an unfussy plant demanding only ordinary good conditions and sunshine. But I feel the gallant dwarf tagetes, remarkably weather resistant, deserve an occasional feed of fertiliser towards the end of the summer.

New introductions arrive season by season so that I hesitate to list them for fear of being out of date by publication day. However, among the dwarf French F_1 Marigolds Golden Nugget, Orange Nugget and Yellow Nugget, famed for their continuous performance throughout the summer, will long be remembered, and we should not forget the Petite varieties (9 in.) neat and spreading dwarfs, orange, lemon yellow, yellow mahogany and tangerine. Meanwhile, Naughty Marietta, 1 ft., with its familiar golden-yellow flowers blotched with maroon, is likely to stay with us for many years to come.

The French and African marigolds are easy to grow but success depends on careful timing, so that the young plants do not become cramped or suffer a check in growth from being held back for fear of frost. Seeds should be sown under glass in February or March or outdoors in late April or May.

Tithonia (Mexican Sunflower). This late-flowering plant has orange-scarlet blooms not unlike that of the zinnia. It seldom flowers until it is tall and mature, and demands a sunny position and a light soil.

Tithonia rotundifolia Torch bears dazzling orange-scarlet flowers on stout 3-ft. stems. It is a showy plant, flowering from August until the frosts arrive.

March sowing in gentle heat will provide plants for planting out in late May or June.

Tobacco Plant, see Nicotiana

Ursinia. This showy South African plant has finely-cut, deep green foliage and masses of brilliant daisy-like, orange flowers with contrasting coloured zones. It is a plant that needs the sun and does well on a sandy soil.

Ursinia anethoides, 1 ft., with orange-yellow, purple-zoned flowers, and *U. versicolour*, 1 ft., bright orange, are the species usually grown, but there are a number of garden hybrids and named varieties for those looking for vivid colour in shades of orange. The flowering period is July to September.

Seeds should be sown in March or April to provide plants for putting out in May.

Venidium (Monarch of the Veldt). Venidium is one of the brightest of the South African annuals with orange daisy-like flowers with striking dark centres. This plant is happy in a sandy soil and sunny position.

Venidium fastuosum, $2\frac{1}{2}$ ft., has large orange flowers with purple-brown zones, 4–5 in. across. The leaves are covered with white hairs giving the foliage a woolly appearance. The *V. fastuosum* hybrids of much the same height vary in colour from orange and yellow to white.

Seeds are sown in March under glass to provide plants for planting out in late May or June. In warm districts outdoor sowings can be made in May where the plants are to flower.

Verbena (Vervain). There are modern strains of verbena in white and shades of mauve, purple, pink and red, some possessing attractive white eyes. These plants enjoy a well-drained soil and sunshine.

The deep violet blue *Verbena canadensis compacta*, blue and white, and *V. erinoides*, 9 in., with fern-like foliage, are desirable plants. The mid-blue Amethyst, which belongs to the *hybrida compacta* group, is free flowering, while the Mammoth hybrids, $1\frac{1}{2}$ ft., have large flowers in purple, blue, red, rose and white. The auricula-eyed strain also offers a good range of colours. They flower from July to September.

Seeds should be sown in February under glass, the seedlings pricked out into boxes as soon as they are large enough to handle and, after hardening off in a cold frame, planted out in May. Verbenas may also be treated as hardy annuals and sown outdoors in May where they are to flower.

Vervain, see Verbena

Zinnia. Modern double-flowered American strains with flowers $4\frac{1}{2}$–5 in. across are available in white, pale and golden yellow, orange, apricot, pink, scarlet, crimson, mauve and purple. Zinnias thrive in full sun and a rich soil that does not dry out in summer.

The many types include the Giant Dahlia-flowered, Giant Chrysanthemum-flowered, Giant Cactus-flowered, $2\frac{1}{2}$ ft., and the Gaillardia-flowered varieties, $1\frac{1}{2}$ ft.; the small-growing Pumilas and Lilliputs, 15 in. and 18 in. tall respectively; and the little Thumbelina Mixed strain, which gives endless flowers in many colours on 6-in. stems. Other attractive dwarfs include the recently introduced Pink and Red Buttons which flower from July to September.

Seeds should be sown in April in boxes under glass. Earlier sowing may necessitate holding young plants back for fear of frosty conditions outdoors, resulting in an unfortunate check in growth. The seedlings should be pricked out as soon as possible and hardened off for planting out during early June. Transplanting must be carried out with care, for zinnias resent being moved.

Below: Viscarias, free-flowering hardy annuals with considerable charm

Annuals for Special Purposes

Annuals for Dry and Sunny Positions

Clarkia	Papaver
Echium	Statice
Eschscholzia	Tagetes
Gazania	Tropaeolum
Lupinus	Venidium
Mesembryanthemum	Zinnia

Annuals That Will Tolerate Damp Positions

Amaranthus	Linaria
Calendula	Linum
Cosmos	Mimulus
Larkspur	Nigella
Limnanthes	Reseda

Annuals That Will Tolerate Partial Shade

Ageratum	Nemophila
Impatiens	Nicotiana
Mimulus	Tropaeolum

Annuals for Balconies and Window Boxes

Ageratum	Nemesia
Alyssum	Petunia
Godetia	*Phlox drummondii*
Iberis	Portulaca
Linaria	Tropaeolum
Lobelia	

Annuals for Beddings

Ageratum	Nemesia
Alyssum	Petunia
Convolvulus tricolor	*Phlox drummondii*
Heliotropium	Tagetes
Impatiens	Verbena
Lobelia	Zinnia

Annuals for Beekeepers

Alyssum maritimum	Nigella
Centaurea	Phacelia
Clarkia	Rudbeckia
Echium	Salvia
Iberis	Scabiosa
Linaria	

Annual Climbers

Cobaea scandens	*Lathyrus odoratus*
Cucurbita (Gourds)	*Tropaeolum majus*
Ipomoea	*Tropaeolum peregrinum*

Annuals for Cutting

Calendula	Matthiola
Delphinium	Nigella
Gaillardia	Salpiglossis
Godetia	Scabiosa
Gypsophila	Viscaria
Lathyrus odoratus	Zinnia

Sweet Scented Annuals

Heliotropium	Matthiola
Lathyrus odoratus	Nicotiana
Lupinus	Reseda

Top left: Gazanias, half-hardy perennials grown as half-hardy annuals
Bottom left: The Twinkle strain of the half-hardy *Phlox drummondii*

Top right: A mixed planting of petunias and nicotianas (Tobacco Plants) below baskets of fuchsias
Bottom right: The colourful, half-hardy *Mesembryanthemum criniflorum*, or Livingstone Daisy

My Choice of Annuals
-for association with other flowers

Flower scent means much to me and I would head
my list with the heavily scented heliotrope,
yellow lupin, stock, tobacco plant, mignonette
and sweet pea. I cherish the miniature old-
fashioned sweet pea, introduced in 1699 and only
recently returned to favour, because of its honey-
suckle fragrance.

The seedsman in his catalogue is apt to credit
a flower with scent when it possesses no more
than an 'insect attracting odour' with which
nature blesses the majority of flowers to guarantee
pollination.

Among the tall plants for the backcloth of the
mixed border there are none more satisfactory
than the verbascums, the Astolat and Pacific,
lilac-pink to raspberry delphiniums, and the pale
yellow oenothera, together with the hollyhocks,
perennial or biennial. In front of these come the
cornflower and sweet sultan, the clarkia, gypsophila, lupin and love-in-a-mist, where they meet
the sweet williams and the globular Shirley
poppies with petals of fascinating and delicate
crepe-paper.

Moving to the fore there are the dazzling
Twinkle and Nana Compacta strains of *Phlox
drummondii*; blocks of Cambridge Blue lobelia and
the many coloured viscaria will not be far away.

Perhaps in your border there will be a hot
corner of orange, tangerine and red–the calendula,
nasturtiums and fiery-coloured South African
annuals–but not in mine! They, together with the
lovely scarlet perennial, *Lobelia cardinalis,* would
find their home against the dark background of
the shrubbery.

For my own part when looking for colour I
prefer the cool to the brash. On the rare occasions
when we get a really hot summer the time
comes when many a gardener will long for foliage
and greenery only–such perennials as euphorbias
and hostas, blue and grey, with perhaps a few

such annuals as the green nicotianas, white
petunias and the Chartreuse-coloured zinnia
Envy, just to break the line.

A place in front of the border would be re-
served for the miniature gilias (formerly known
as leptosiphons) with tiny gay pincushion flowers
in almost every colour.

When it comes to climbers I would settle for
Cobaea scandens, the exotic Cup-and-Saucer
Plant in blue and green, and the brilliant *Ipomoea*
Heavenly Blue (Morning Glory) competing with
the blue of the sky.

Part Three

Biennials

*Cultivation of
Biennial Flowers*

*A Choice
of Biennials*

Bottom left: Double hollyhocks, *Althaea* Chater's
Double Mixed
Bottom right: Single, mixed blooms of the charming
Canterbury Bell

Left: Foxgloves, the stately flowers which give a good
performance on the poorest of soil

Cultivation of Biennials

Biennials are grown in the same way as annuals but take two years to accomplish the life cycle that the annual completes in one year. The true biennial makes generous growth the first year and flowers and says farewell the second year.

Many attractive perennials, hardy, half-hardy and some slightly tender, are apt to grow leggy and untidy when mature and are more successfully grown as biennials. Among these are the hollyhocks, sweet williams, and wallflowers. Gardeners who have kept their wallflowers for a third year will have noticed that the plants become less uniform and flower less their second flowering season. But the defining line between annual and biennial is almost non-existent in the case of some plants such as the East Lothian Stock, a biennial, that if treated as an annual will flower the same year as it is sown.

Early-flowering biennials are popular with gardeners interested in bedding plants as they can be discarded after spring flowering and replaced in good time by summer bedders. And indeed, there is no better companion for the tulip than the Forget-me-Not. Although playing an important part both in the annual and perennial border, the biennial is seldom given a border to itself.

Biennials should be sown $\frac{1}{2}$ in. deep and about 8–9 in. apart in late May or early June choosing a shady or semi-shady spot. When the seedlings reach 2–3 in. they may be transplanted to a nursery bed in an open position, about 5 in. apart. This intermediate move is advised as it encourages strength and bushiness. In the autumn the plants should be installed in their flowering positions. This last move should not be delayed otherwise the plants will not have time to establish themselves before the winter.

Biennials are vulnerable to disease when in the seedling stage, particularly when under glass, and care should be taken to give adequate ventilation.

133

A Choice of Biennials

Althaea (Hollyhock). This plant is a hardy, short-lived perennial but it is best grown as a biennial and strains for growing as half-hardy annuals are available. Young plants should be raised every year when possible and a little cosseting will be well rewarded. Hollyhocks give a good performance on the poorest of land, but, like other plants, respond to good fare. All are 6–9 ft. tall.

Chater's Improved and the newer Powder Puffs are both bright and admirable strains but there is much pleasure to be had from a sixpenny packet of ordinary singles.

Sowings may be made in June or July outdoors to provide flowering plants for the following year. If they are to be grown as annuals, seeds should be sown under glass in February or March to provide plants for setting out in the border in late April, after hardening off.

Campanula. The biennials include some of the best campanulas. *Campanula pyramidalis,* the Chimney Bellflower, a perennial better grown as a biennial, is an impressive plant with long spikes crowded with blue starry bells—or white in the excellent variety *alba.* This tall plant—4–5 ft. in height—enjoys a warm border, careful staking and a sheltered position.

The Canterbury Bell (*C. medium* and its varieties), 2½–3 ft., one of my favourite 'cup-and-saucer' plants, is to be had in many shades of blue, rose-pink and white. There are double, semi-double and single varieties and dwarfs for small gardens or pot growing.

Seeds should be sown in a sunny bed in June and the resulting seedlings thinned out to 6 in. apart. The plants can then be moved to their flowering positions in early autumn.

Cheiranthus (Wallflower). There are many varieties of wallflower in shades of yellow, chestnut red, crimson and purple-mauve—all deliciously scented. Wallflowers prefer a well-drained, not too heavy soil which contains a little

lime or mortar rubble. They must be firmly planted and firmed up after severe frost. When the plants are well established leading growths may be pinched out to encourage a bushy habit. Wallflowers benefit from watering in dry weather.

Cheiranthus allionii, commonly known as the Siberian Wallflower, bears deep orange or yellow flowers on 1-ft. stems. It comes into bloom in May on the heels of the Wallflower proper but, alas, lacks the latter's lovely scent.

Varieties of the Wallflower (*C. cheiri*), fiery and ruby red, sometimes almost scarlet, gold, orange salmon, primrose, pink and mauve, grow from 1 –2 ft. and all are deliciously scented.

Seed should be sown in May and June, and the resulting seedlings transplanted in early autumn. Sowing may be done in boxes placed in a cold frame or in the open ground. The seed should be sown as thinly as possible. The seedlings should be moved at least once before they reach their flowering positions in October or November, the earlier the better, giving the plants time to make a good root system before winter sets in.

Cotton Thistle, see Onopordon

Dianthus (Sweet William). It is not easy to define members of this large family as biennials or half-hardy annuals, but it is worth noting that the Chinese or Indian pinks, biennial in character, can be successfully grown as annuals while a number of carnations, border, dwarf or picotee, may be grown as biennial or perennial. Sown from May to July they will flower the following summer.

The Sweet William, varieties of *Dianthus barbatus,* is one of the belles of the group. With flowers of scarlet, crimson, pink, harlequin or white, it is superb. Like all members of this genus it appreciates a place in the sun and a well-drained alkaline soil.

The Sweet William is most satisfactorily raised from sowings made in a cold frame in May, the seedlings being transplanted first to a nursery bed

Top: The Siberian Wallflower, *Cheiranthus allionii*, with deep orange or yellow flowers
Bottom: The Sweet William, *Dianthus barbatus*, one of the belles of the dianthus family

and later on, in September or October, to their flowering positions. Sowings can also be made outdoors in June or July, pricking out the seedlings as soon as they can be handled and moving them to their flowering positions in September.

Digitalis (Foxglove). The Foxglove is a biennial or short-lived perennial. It is easily grown in light loamy or leafy soil in an open or partially shaded border. The purple form has been succeeded by the Excelsior Strain, 4–5 ft., with flowers of cream, primrose, pink and purple, meticulously spotted and blotched with maroon; the flowers are carried horizontally all round the stem. The Foxy strain, 3 ft., can be grown as a biennial or half-hardy annual and has flowers in shades of carmine, pink, cream and white spotted maroon.

Seeds should be sown outdoors in May or June in a well-prepared seed bed and the seedlings pricked out into a partially shaded nursery bed when large enough to handle.

Evening Primrose, see Oenothera
Forget-Me-Not, see Myosotis
Foxglove, see Digitalis
Gilia (Texas Plume or Standing Cypress). The beautiful biennial, *Gilia rubra* (syn. *G. coronopifolia*), deserves mention. The flowers are of a rich and rather rare red in colour, and the foliage is finely cut. The plants grow to about 3 ft.

Although it is a biennial and can be treated as such, it can also be grown as an annual, seed being sown in January or February in a temperature of 16°C. (60°F.) and the young plants put out in May where many will flower from July to October.

Hesperis (Sweet Rocket). This perennial is usually grown more successfully as a biennial. The varieties of *Hesperis matronalis*, 2–3 ft., have single and double flowers in shades of mauve, purple and white. *H. tristis*, 1½ ft., has forms with white to cream and red to purple flowers, and is said to be sweet scented in the evening.

Seeds should be sown in May or June for flowering the following year.

Hollyhock, see Althaea
Honesty, see Lunaria

The silvery foliage of the Cotton Thistle,
Onoporodon arabicum

Iceland Poppy, see Papaver

Lunaria (Moonwort, Honesty). This decorative biennial bears silvery-headed, moon-shaped seed pods for drying and winter decoration. These should be cut soon after their outer covering has been discarded and before they are disfigured by the rain. Honesty is happy in ordinary garden soil and grows well in sun or semi-shade.

Lunaria annua (syn. *L. biennis*), 1½–2 ft., has violet-purple flowers and there are varieties with white and purple flowers.

Seeds should be sown outdoors in May or June.

Matthiola (Stock). The East Lothian and Brompton Stocks, 1½ ft. or taller, do well treated as biennials. They come true from seed in a lovely range of colours, pink, carmine, magenta, mauve, purple, creamy yellow and white. There are single and double stocks and the gardener must be prepared to accept, for genetic reasons, a number of singles from the double stock packet. (Although if the dark seedlings of Hanson's 100 per cent double stocks are discarded, singles should be reduced to a minimum.) They will flower in early summer.

Stocks enjoy good fare, thrive on chalk, and are often seen at their best at the seaside. They need plenty of light and should not be allowed to go dry through the summer.

When happy in their surroundings stocks will, on occasion, over-winter and reach 4 ft. or so in their second season giving a fine performance.

Seeds should be sown in a frame in June or July in the case of Brompton Stocks and July or August for East Lothian Stocks, and the resulting seedlings pricked out into a frame as soon as possible. They should be over-wintered in a frame and planted out in April; only in mild areas should they be planted out in September *in situ*.

Meconopsis. Some species of *Meconopsis* are best treated as biennials, for they are temperamental subjects needing constant attention throughout their life. Care must be taken in pricking out and handling seedlings. If young plants are planted too deeply they are liable to damp off. Meconopsis enjoy a deep, cool, leafy or peat soil preferably rather acid, and partial shade.

Meconopsis integrifolia, the Chinese Yellow Poppy, with large pale yellow flowers dies after flowering and must be constantly replaced by seed. It grows up to 3 ft. *M. napaulensis* (syn. *M. wallichii*), the Satin Poppy, variable in colour from red to purple-blue, claret and yellow, is ideal for a moist, shaded position. The foliage is hairy and handsome, and the plant grows to 4–8 ft.

Seeds should be sown very thinly in a shaded frame in May or June. Seedlings should be treated with respect and be given individual pots when large enough to handle. They should be planted out in September where they are to flower.

Moonwort, see Lunaria

Mullein, see Verbascum

Myosotis (Forget-me-not). The myosotis are

136

perennials in blue, pink and white with a yellow eye, usually grown as biennials. The plants should be kept moist and planted out as early in the autumn as possible. The majority of the garden forms are derived from *M. alpestris* and make enchanting spring bedders, and there is an excellent choice of varieties to be found in the seedsman's catalogue.

Plants are easily raised from seed sown in May or June; the resulting seedlings can be transplanted into beds in October to flower during the following year. The Forget-me-not invariably perpetuates itself.

Oenothera (Evening Primrose). *Oenothera biennis* is the common species grown so easily that it stands in danger of being looked upon as a weed. The flowers open only in the evening. It is easily pleased and does well in light shade.

Seeds should be sown in May and June, the resulting seedlings being thinned out as soon as possible and the plants moved to their flowering positions in September.

Onopordon (Cotton Thistle). This blue-purple-flowered perennial is frequently treated as a biennial. Its splendid spiny, silver foliage covered with fine white hair and its silver bracts make it a dramatic plant in a large border. It thrives in light soil in a sunny position.

The two species worth noting are *O. acanthium*, the Cotton Thistle, 4 ft., and *O. arabicum*, with magnificent branching stems and large decorative flowers, 6–8 ft.

Seeds should be sown in May or June and the resulting seedlings thinned out as soon as possible. They should be transferred to their flowering quarters in September.

Pansy, see Viola

Papaver (Iceland Poppy). *Papaver nudicaule*, with a height range of 12–18 in., grows well if treated as a biennial (see also p. 79). Plants must be well grown and robust if they are to flower satisfactorily.

Papaver Champagne Bubbles is a large-flowered strain in good colours. There are now scarlet, tangerine, cerise-pink and rose forms, some frilly-edged, and borne on good stout stems. Double forms are also available. The flowers are useful for cutting.

Seeds should be sown in May or June, the young plants being placed in their flowering positions in the autumn. Iceland Poppies can also be treated as annuals, sowing seeds under glass in February or March.

Standing Cypress, see Gilia
Stock, see Matthiola
Sweet Rocket, see Hesperis
Sweet William, see Dianthus
Texas Plume, see Gilia
Verbascum (Mullein). Many of the verbascums are hardy biennials. The yellow or sulphur-coloured flower spikes mounting from silver-grey rosettes are extremely decorative. The Mulleins enjoy the sun and a rich soil. The strong spikes do not require staking.

Verbascum bombyciferum (syn. *V. Broussa*), an amusing sulphur-yellow giant (of 6 ft.) covered with dense grey plush wool, soft as velvet, has a comic appearance. In fact it is the downy practical joke of the border. *V. hybridum* Harkness Hybrid has huge yellow flowers while *V. h.* Miss Willmott is a handsome white variety.

Seed should be sown in May or June in the garden and the seedlings thinned out as soon as it can be safely done. The plants should be transferred to their flowering quarters in September.

Viola (Pansy). The Pansies are often best grown as biennials being sown in summer in a cold frame, if available, and moved to their final positions in the autumn for flowering in the following year. It is important to keep the seedlings moist, particularly when transplanting.

The winter-flowering pansies have become extremely popular and it is pleasant to be able to pick a few blooms in January or February.

Seeds should be sown in a cold frame in June or July and the resulting seedlings pricked out into boxes or pots as soon as they can be safely handled. The young plants should be put outdoors in September.

Wallflower, see Cheiranthus

Index

Abbreviation: p = photograph